THE POWER OF WRITING

DARTMOUTH '66

IN THE TWENTY-FIRST CENTURY

the Power *of* Writing

EDITED BY Christiane Donahue

AND Kelly Blewett

Dartmouth College Press   Hanover, New Hampshire

Dartmouth College Press
An imprint of University Press of New England
www.upne.com
CC 2015 Trustees of Dartmouth College

Manufactured in the United States of America
Designed by Mindy Basinger Hill
Typeset in Parkinson Electra Pro

For permission to reproduce any of the material in this
book, contact Permissions, University Press of New England,
One Court Street, Suite 250, Lebanon NH 03766; or visit
www.upne.com

Library of Congress Cataloging-in-Publication Data

The power of writing: Dartmouth '66 in the twenty-first century /
Christiane Donahue and Kelly Blewett, Editors.
       pages   cm
ISBN 978-1-61168-762-0 (cloth: alk. paper)—
ISBN 978-1-61168-739-2 (pbk.: alk. paper)—
ISBN 978-1-61168-740-8 (ebook)
1. English language—Rhetoric—Study and teaching (Higher)
2. Academic writing—Study and teaching (Higher)
I. Donahue, Christiane, editor. II. Blewett, Kelly, editor.

PE1404.P619 2015
808'.0420711—dc23   2014038230

contents

MICHAEL MASTANDUNO

foreword The Power of Writing

This volume represents the individual and interactive thinking that came out of the 2012 Writing Summit at Dartmouth College. The summit honored the forty-fifth anniversary of Dartmouth's original seminar on the teaching of writing, in 1966. That now-legendary three-week gathering, officially called the Anglo-American Conference on the Teaching and Learning of English but widely known as the Dartmouth Seminar, launched an ongoing dialogue on language and methodology, established broader definitions of "English," modernized the curriculum, and led to a shift in thinking about writing — from prescribed product to expressive process. Albert Kitzhaber, the keynote speaker and driver of the US focus at the seminar, had done groundbreaking work at Dartmouth in the years leading up to the seminar, studying errors in students' writing and analyzing the general first-year curriculum. The seminar's US, UK, and Canadian participants set out lines of inquiry that we continue to pursue today: the role of technology in writing; the attention to writing processes and to understanding how writers write, not just what they write; the interaction between speech and writing; and the shifting nature of so-called standard English.

The Dartmouth Seminar cemented the establishment of a scholarly field dedicated to understanding, researching, and teaching writing in higher education: the field of composition and rhetoric. The seminar also inspired the writing across the curriculum (WAC) and writing in the disciplines movements in the United States. And it created the foundation for a key shift in the 1970s and 1980s from understanding meaning as existing independent of writing to understanding it as socially constructed through writing.

The 2012 Writing Summit was intended to further the process of examining and discussing writing and the teaching of writing in relation to disciplinary knowledge. The contributions in this volume grow out of the encounters at the summit among leading voices in writing in the sciences, social sciences, humanities, and interdisciplinary studies, with responses by outstanding Dartmouth faculty members from the same disciplinary perspectives and top scholars in the field of writing studies. The trios of talks that are presented in this volume's parts were each designed to offer insights from three perspectives on the power, shape, form, construction, and impact of writing in the world. The framing introductory talk detailed the history of the original Dartmouth Seminar and brought its concerns into the twenty-first century; the closing forum allowed for interactive questioning among all speakers and the audience of writing's norms, conventions, integral role in disciplinary meaning making, and unique power in communicating that meaning to the world.

Dartmouth and the field of writing studies now look forward to the fiftieth anniversary of the Dartmouth Seminar in 2016 as a moment for reflection and looking ahead to the future of writing research and instruction.

JOSEPH HARRIS

introduction Updating Dartmouth

The aim of the 2012 Writing Summit at Dartmouth College was to revisit some of the issues raised at a much earlier meeting at the college: the 1966 Anglo-American Conference on the Teaching and Learning of English, commonly known as the Dartmouth Seminar. This earlier meeting had become famous, at least among college writing teachers, as a moment when a new view of writing and its teaching began to emerge. Almost fifty years later, our hope at the 2012 summit was to rethink what had by now become a set of axioms for the teaching of writing, to see how we might update or revise the ideas of 1966.

My task was to provide a historical context for that work. In my book, *A Teaching Subject* (Harris 2012), I offer a detailed account of the debates that took place at Dartmouth in 1966. Rather than simply rehashing here what I've already said there, I'd like instead to briefly note some lessons we can still take away from those debates, before going on to point to some new problems and opportunities that we now face.

The Lessons of Dartmouth

The full title of the 1966 meeting was the Anglo-American Conference on the Teaching and Learning of English at Dartmouth College. The terms in that long title merit some attention.

Anglo-American: Although in 1966 English was already well on its way to becoming a global language, the focus of the conference rarely strayed beyond England and America. All of the participants came from Great Britain or the United States (there was one "observer" from Canada); most were males; and, as far as I can tell, all were white.

Seminar: Though called a conference, the 1966 meeting was truly conceived of as a seminar, a site for the discussion of new work and new ideas. It was not a conference or convention; it did not aim for or achieve consensus. Rather, a remarkable number of books and articles — some official, some not — came out of the meeting, and most were openly argumentative. It was not a feel-good event; its lessons appear in the form of conflicts rather than agreements.

Teaching: Most of the participants, from both the British and American delegations, were teacher-educators. They were thus more interested in English as a teaching subject in the schools than in literary criticism, rhetoric, or linguistics per se.

Learning: As teachers, many participants at Dartmouth showed a strong interest in the work of students. There's a democratic and populist feel to many of the books and articles that came out of the conference. Student texts were quoted often, and with respect.

English: Many of the ideas that came out of Dartmouth in 1966 still influence how writing is taught in college. Ironically, though, few of the participants at Dartmouth would have identified themselves as writing teachers. They were, for the most part, teachers of English — which is to say, literature, and which they tended to define in fairly traditional terms. But the reason that Dartmouth continues to have an impact on college teaching has little to do with what was said there about the study of English literature. That is, at best, a guild concern. The ideas from Dartmouth that matter today are those about how to help students learn to use language more effectively and expressively — that is, about how to teach writing. (Note that we convened in 2012 a summit not on English but on writing.) In that sense, the most lasting impact of the 1966 Dartmouth conference was almost accidental.

So what were those ideas about writing and teaching? Perhaps it might be more accurate to speak in terms of attitudes. Scholars at Dartmouth like James Britton (from the United Kingdom) and James Moffett (from the United States) were more interested in the everyday uses of language than in literary forms or genres. They thus analyzed not only texts by famous authors but also themes, papers, poems, and journal entries by students and other ordinary people. Both Britton and Moffett were especially interested in ways of supporting the growth of students as writers. Each thus argued, in his own particular style, for a curriculum that began with personal and expressive writing and moved outward to more public and analytic forms.

Not everyone at Dartmouth agreed with this emphasis on personal growth and the practice of writing. Indeed, in the keynote address at the conference, Albert Kitzhaber of the University of Oregon called for a more coherent and well-articulated definition of English as "an organized body of knowledge with an integrity of its own" (1966, 12). Essentially he saw the problem facing the conference as one of defining and ordering what needed to be taught in the name of English — something along the lines of the scaffolded curricula of many of the sciences. Responding to Kitzhaber, Britton offered a radically different view of English as not a conventional discipline but rather "the integrating area of all public knowledge" (1966, 12). To illustrate, he offered this remarkable metaphor: "My mother used to make jam tarts and she used to roll out the pastry and I remember this very well —

I can still feel what it is like to do it, although I have never done it since. She used to roll out the pastry and then she took a glass and cut out a jam tart, then cut out another jam tart. Well we have cut out geography, and we have cut out history, and we have cut out science. What do we cut out for English? I suggest that we don't. I suggest that is what is left. That is the rest of it" (12).

The tension between these two views of English — as a discipline or as a kind of metadiscipline, "an integrating area" — drove the rest of the work of the 1966 conference. The debate about the two views was unusually intelligent and spirited, but has an inside-baseball quality if you are not already invested in the question of what the ideal structure of English studies should be. Still, two points strike me as worth making about this debate. The first, however banal it may seem, is that there is something to both sides of the argument. There are real things to teach students about literary genres, figures, and traditions and also about the forms of expository and imaginative writing. But those things become valuable only when students put them to use in their own work. I suspect there are similar tensions between content and practice in other fields.

The second point is more important. In suggesting that English is "what is left," what connects the work that goes on in the various disciplines, Britton laid the groundwork for the teaching of writing across the curriculum. For although it may take different forms in different fields, writing is something that all academics do, which in turn suggests that helping students develop as writers should be a core part of undergraduate study throughout the disciplines. This emphasis spoke to a growing number of teachers in us colleges in the 1960s who were beginning to experiment with teaching writing as a process — through the use of free writing and journals, writing-to-learn exercises, and small-group workshops.

In the years after the Dartmouth conference, the work of Britton and Moffett was increasingly invoked by such teachers and scholars. Growth met process. Moffett's *Teaching the Universe of Discourse* (1968) outlined a scheme for gradually moving students from informal to public forms of writing, while in *The Development of Writing Abilities* (1975), a report on an extensive study of the kinds of writing done in British schools, Britton and his coauthors documented the intellectual aridity of efforts to simply teach models of academic discourse. Far more than the official reports on the conference, these two books caught the spirit of change that emanated from Dartmouth with their enthusiastic interest in everyday uses of language, in writing as a means of making knowledge, in how texts actually are produced, and in the work of students and teachers. These values resonate as powerfully today as in 1966.

Moving Forward

However, the circumstances of our work have clearly changed. One way to get at some of the differences between 1966 and today is to look at one of the few photographs we possess of the Dartmouth conference (figure 1.1).

The photo shows an appealing but remarkably homogeneous group. Everyone is white, and I count only three women. Almost everyone appears to be middle-aged and middle class. There's a lot of paper — books, folders, and notepads — but no sign of any other media. We know that no disciplines other than English were represented, and that all of the participants were citizens of the United States or the United Kingdom.

It is hard to imagine taking a similar photo today. The composition of the group in the room would be different. The students we work with identify with a wide range of ethnicities, cultures,

FIGURE I.1 "1966 Dartmouth Seminar," David Pierce Studio, 1966. Photograph, Rauner Special Collections Library, Sanborn, Dartmouth College.

classes, and nations — and we now better understand the need to reflect that diversity in our professional meetings and journals. At Dartmouth in 2012, both Hortense Spillers and Melanie Benson Taylor spoke movingly about how writing as women and people of color has influenced the work they've done. These were simply not salient issues for most of the men gathered at Dartmouth in 1966. The essays in this volume by Spillers and Taylor also show an especially happy result of this impulse to reflect on how a writer's position in the culture can act to shape what she is able to say — which is an emerging genre of academic prose that is highly personal, nuanced, and engaged.

The 1966 conference also failed to confront the growing use of English as a global language. Instead, as John Trimbur (2008) points out, the papers and books from Dartmouth routinely assumed that students were native speakers of English. There was almost no discussion of how to teach multilingual or international students. And although everyone wanted to help students claim a stronger voice in their culture — indeed, there is a quiet class animus to much of the talk at Dartmouth that I find bracing — that culture was imagined in traditional and nationalistic terms as, well, "Anglo-American." But if it was ever true at any time that most writing students were the heirs of Bacon and Emerson, that is surely not the case now. Writing in English is taught in schools around the globe, sometimes to students whose first language is English, but often not. And in US universities, writing teachers routinely work with students who count English as only one of several languages that they speak and who have little need or desire to identify with traditional Anglo-American culture. We need to find ways of imagining multilingualism as a strength, not a problem, as we teach writing in a global and hybrid culture.

Katherine Bergeron brings these issues into sharp relief at the 2012 Writing Summit in her brilliant essay in this volume on the difficulties of writing about *la mélodie française*, a vocal musical form of the early 1900s. Bergeron offers a striking example of how a writer can exploit the possibilities of a multilingual, multimodal, transnational age. She translates the physical experience of listening to (and playing) music into prose, shifting fluidly from English to French and from an analysis of the intonations and emphases of a vocal performance to the rhythms and meters of poetic verse and the playing of piano. Yet it also seems to me that the very delicacy and nuance of her interpretations — as when she points out the meaning of the emphasis that a certain singer gives to the unvoiced *e* in French — depend on, and contribute to, a quite specific tradition of academic music criticism. She is speaking, that is, to a clearly defined set of fellow specialists, working firmly within a particular intellectual tradition, as she also draws on the new resources of a global, digital culture.

I say all this not in criticism but admiration. Still, I am grateful for Maria Jerskey's response to Bergeron in this volume, in which she raises the question of what it means to teach writing *outside* of a single, well-defined culture or intellectual tradition — that is, of how to teach students to write across cultures and disciplines. I'm not sure that any of us knows yet how to do just that. But I am convinced that, as we move further into the twenty-first century, our job will be not simply to teach students to write within a particular discipline or culture but to move among and across them. The 1966 Dartmouth conference offers us little guidance about how to do that.

Coincidentally, the most significant attempt so far to update the ideas of Dartmouth also began at a meeting in New Hampshire. In 1994 a small group of scholars met in New London to talk about the future of literacy teaching in an age of rapid globalization and technological change. Two years later, what had by then become known as the New London Group published a manifesto called "A Pedagogy of Multiliteracies" in the *Harvard Educational Review*. A few years later, the group enlisted the help of scholars from Africa, Australia, Great Britain, and the United States to elaborate on that pedagogy in a collection of essays on teaching titled *Multiliteracies* (Cope and Kalantzis 2000b).

The concerns driving the work of the New London Group were succinctly captured by Bill Cope and Mary Kalantzis in their introduction to *Multiliteracies*. Playing on the name of the small and picturesque New England town where the group first met, they noted: "Now one billion people speak that difficult and messy little language, English, spoken four centuries ago by only about a million or so people in the vicinity of London, old London. The story of the language, and the story of the last few centuries, including its many injustices, is the story of many new Londons. This issue — how the language meets with cultural and linguistic diversity — was one of our main concerns" (2000a, 3). It's a compelling idea — that we now work and study in a world of many new Londons, of constantly emerging and evolving uses of English. And surely these changes in language have been driven in large part by the recent explosion of new technologies of communication. Although the New London Group didn't argue for particular uses of new media in teaching, they did urge writing teachers to respond to the accelerating rate of change in the ways we communicate, and to the new kinds of texts we now read and compose. They were also acutely aware that studying or teaching English no longer involves, if it ever fully did, identifying with a stable Anglo-American culture — in other words, that we now routinely teach in the midst of remarkable diversity.

Where the New London Group was most prescient, however, was in viewing technological change and cultural diversity as aspects of the same phenomenon of globalization. This explains their use of the term "multiliteracies": literacies are multiple because of the increasing range of media — print, graphic, sonic, and digital — that writers now have ready access to. But literacies are also multiple because more and more writers bring the resources of diverse cultures and languages to their work. This led the New London Group to argue for replacing an insistence on teaching standard written forms with a focus on the expressive possibilities of what they called the new "technologies of meaning" (1996, 64).

In short, we now teach in circumstances in which change and hybridity are the norm. This has led to a growing interest in how the uses of writing shift from one context to the next — public, personal, formal, informal, in the community, on the job, and in the various disciplines of the academy. Scholars like Britton and Moffett redirected our focus from static forms and genres of writing to how language is actually used in the world. But they had little to say about the social contexts of language use. And the 1966 conference was silent on the question of disciplinarity. The English classroom was its world.

Things were different in 2012. The Writing Summit invited scholars from math, linguistics, cognitive science, history, music, Native American studies, cultural studies, literature, and composition to Dartmouth to talk about the roles and uses of writing in their work. There was no set format for our presentations. Some of us spoke more or less extemporaneously; others read from prepared texts. Some made extensive use of the Internet and digital media; others depended on paper and voice alone. Indeed, one of the issues we most disagreed about was whether we should be talking with or reading to each other — with, for the most part, the scientists preferring a more casual mode of presentation and the humanists a more scripted performance. But it seems to me that this very question — How should we talk together? — takes us a step beyond Dartmouth 1966 in acknowledging the new uncertainty and dynamism of our situation. We have augmented the range of ways — print, online, audio, and video — we can communicate and connect with each other at the very same time that many of our publics and readerships seem to be splintering away from one another. The aim of the 2012 Writing Summit at Dartmouth was, according to the program, to explore "the power of writing in the contemporary world." I think the most important thing we discovered was that writing is no longer a single thing, with a particular force or power, but rather a tool whose uses vary widely from one context to the next and from one discipline to another.

REFERENCES

Britton, James. 1966. "Response to Working Party Paper No. 1. — What Is English?" In *What Is English, Working Party Paper No. 1; Response, Report to the Seminar, and Supporting Papers One*

through Six. http://www.eric.ed.gov/contentdelivery/servlet
/ERICServlet?accno=ED082201.

Britton, James, Tony Burgess, Nancy Martin, Alex McLeod, and Harold
Rosen. 1975. *The Development of Writing Abilities.* London: Macmillan.

Cope, Bill, and Mary Kalantzis. 2000a. "Multiliteracies: The Beginnings
of an Idea." In *Multiliteracies: Literacy Learning and the Design of
Social Futures,* edited by Bill Cope and Mary Kalantzis, 3–8. New York:
Routledge.

Cope, Bill, and Mary Kalantzis, eds. 2000b. *Multiliteracies: Literacy
Learning and the Design of Social Futures.* New York: Routledge.

Harris, Joseph. 2012. *A Teaching Subject: Composition since 1966.* New ed.
Logan: Utah State University Press.

Kitzhaber, Albert. 1966. "Working Party Paper No. 1: What Is English?"
In *What Is English, Working Party Paper No. 1; Response, Report to
the Seminar, and Supporting Papers One through Six.* http://www.eric
.ed.gov/contentdelivery/servlet/ERICServlet?accno=ED082201.

Moffett, James. 1968. *Teaching the Universe of Discourse.* Boston: Houghton Mifflin.

New London Group. 1996. "A Pedagogy of Multiliteracies: Designing Social Futures." *Harvard Educational Review* 66, no. 1: 6–92.

Trimbur, John. 2008. "The Dartmouth Conference and the Geohistory of
the Native Speaker." *College English* 71, no. 2: 142–69.

part 1 Sciences

STEVEN STROGATZ

one Writing about Math for the Perplexed and the Traumatized

In the summer of 2009 I received an unexpected e-mail message from David Shipley, the editor of the op-ed page in the *New York Times*. He invited me to look him up next time I was in the city and said there was something he'd like to discuss.

Over lunch at the Oyster Bar restaurant in Grand Central Station, he asked whether I'd ever have time to write a series about the elements of math, aimed at people like him. He said he'd majored in English in college and hadn't studied math since high school. At some point he'd lost his way and given up. Although he could usually do what his math teachers had asked of him, he'd never really seen the point of it. Later in life he'd been puzzled to hear math described as beautiful. Could I convey some of that beauty to his readers — many of whom, he suspected, were as lost he was?

I was thrilled by his proposition. I love math, but even more I love trying to explain it.

Relax — I'll spare you my math lessons. But I would like to touch on a few of the writing challenges that this opportunity entailed, along with the goals I set for myself, and then describe how, by borrowing from three great science writers, I tried to meet those challenges. I'm not sure if any of my suggestions will be valuable to writers working in other technical fields, but I suspect they might.

Three Challenges

One challenge in writing about math is that the subject is inherently abstract. The objects of mathematics are disembodied ideas, not people or stories or things. Although its simplest concepts — numbers and shapes — aren't too hard for most readers to grasp, math becomes increasingly slippery and ethereal as we move on to formulas and functions, theorems and proofs, derivatives and integrals.

Then there's the matter of the strange symbols and jargon. All of mathematics after grade-school arithmetic is written in letters, not numbers, and sometimes in Greek. Its terminology is unfamiliar and, to the uninitiated, unpronounceable. Can you say $\int$? And what on earth is a directrix or — worse yet — a latus rectum?

Finally, attention must be paid to the psychiatric dimensions of the subject. Math is linked in the popular mind with phobia and anxiety. You'd think we were discussing spiders. So anyone hoping to write about math for a wide audience needs to reckon with the reality that math is, for many people, terrifying. Boring. Meaningless. And, in the most extreme cases, all of the above.

Three Audiences

After years of listening to people's emotional stories about their experiences with math, I've come to recognize three broad groups into which all of humanity falls (I'm kidding, of course, but not entirely):

1) *The traumatized:* These folks suffered humiliation somewhere along the line, maybe as early as second or third grade when they were subjected to the arcana of borrowing and carry-

ing. Or maybe they hit the wall at long division, word problems, or linear algebra. In any case, for these wounded souls, math is now an unhappy memory, a lasting blow to the ego: "I'm just not a math person." "I don't have a head for numbers." "I loved math until I got to [insert tricky math concept here]." Other subjects can inflict the same kind of damage, but not to the same degree and not quite so painfully as math does.

2) *The perplexed:* This is David Shipley's camp. For him and his ilk, math left no scars; it merely felt pointless. These are the people who never quite knew what they were doing mathematically, yet they compensated by working hard, following directions, and overcoming failures. A large proportion of successful people fall into this camp — essentially anyone who wasn't a natural at math.

3) *The naturals:* Though it's taboo to admit it, I believe there are some kids who have a feel for math. It makes sense to them and gives them pleasure and satisfaction. They may or may not get good grades; that depends more on how hard they work and how well they play the game of school. But the talent is there. In rare cases, they grow up to become mathematicians. Or they may go into a related field: accounting, engineering, computers, finance, medicine, and so on. Or, most likely of all, they never use math again after they join the workforce. Nonetheless, they retain a lifelong affection for it. These are the people who used to read Martin Gardner's "Mathematical Games" column in *Scientific American.* Almost all books, blogs, and magazine articles on so-called popular math are directed toward them, and them alone.

That's why, as crude as this classification scheme may be, it's useful. It helps us see that groups 1 and 2 — the traumatized and the perplexed — are underserved mathematically. Though David Shipley didn't put it this way, he was asking me to write for them.

The Need for Empathy

Whether I'm teaching a class, tutoring one on one, writing for my colleagues in other scientific disciplines, or trying to convey the beauty of math to the wider public, I've learned that explaining math successfully is not mainly about the logic and clarity of the explanation. (Sorry, Mr. Spock.) Explaining math well requires empathy. The explainer needs to recognize that there's another person on the receiving end of the explanation. This may be obvious to anyone other than a mathematician. But in our world, an all-too-common approach is to state the assumptions, state the theorems, prove the theorems, and stop. Any questions?

What makes this approach so ineffective is that it answers questions the student hasn't thought to ask. On top of that, it can be exhausting to follow someone else's train of thought. A captive audience of students has no choice, of course; they're forced to listen and yield. That's how we, as math teachers, get in the habit of forgetting to empathize.

If you want someone to follow your mathematical disquisitions voluntarily — or, better yet, happily — you have to help him or her love the questions you're asking. This is true for any audience but especially for the traumatized and the perplexed. *You have to help them love the questions.*

But how?

Three Routes to Mathematical Seduction

For any would-be pop math writer, here are a few surefire techniques.

(1) Illuminate. Give the reader a shiver of pleasure by providing an "Aha!" experience. (2) Make connections. Tie the math to something the reader already enjoys. (3) Treat the reader like a friend of yours — a nonmathematical friend. Then you'll instinctively do everything right.

In what follows, I'll try to flesh out what I mean by these techniques and show how three giants of science writing — Richard Feynman, Stephen Jay Gould, and Lewis Thomas — served as inspirations of mine.

PROVIDE ILLUMINATION

Moments of illumination help a reader fall in love with math, especially after struggling in the dark for so long.

The illumination can be purely verbal. In one of my articles, I pointed out why fractions like 2/3 or 1/4 are called "rational numbers" — they involve ratios of whole numbers. This struck my wife, Carole, as an epiphany. She had always labored under the misimpression that rational numbers were somehow more reasonable than irrational numbers, but she could never see what was so flighty or hysterical about the latter. Now she understood. Irrational numbers are simply those that can't be expressed as a ratio of two whole numbers. They're ir-ratio-nal.

Another revelation for her had to do with the word "squared." No teacher had ever bothered to explain why "2 squared" is synonymous with 2 times 2, or "3 squared" with 3 times 3. It's because a collection of 4 or 9 objects can be arranged as a 2 by 2 or 3 by 3 square shape, like this (figure 1.1):

On other occasions in the series, I tried to illuminate the reasoning behind mathematical statements that all of us heard in

FIGURE 1.1

school, but that few of us ever really understood, like why a negative times a negative is a positive, or where the formula for the area of the circle comes from.

MAKE CONNECTIONS

Math becomes more appealing when it's tied to topics the reader cares about. Sports, music, literature, movies, science, business, law — they're all great sources of math in action. For anyone who likes to get physical, vectors seem a lot more vivid when they're illustrated by samba dance steps or how Roger Federer hits his running forehand down the line. For history buffs, the rules for multiplying negative and positive numbers come to life when you show how much sense they can make of the shifting alliances among European countries in the run-up to World War I.

Math sheds light on many other mysteries, large and small. Here's one that all of us have wondered about: When you're buying clothes on sale, does it save you more money if the clerk applies the discount first and then adds the sales tax to the reduced price? Or would it be cheaper for you the other way around? (Answer: It doesn't matter; the commutative law of multiplication shows why.)

Making the effort to include real-world connections like these sends a message to the reader: Even if you are not primarily interested in math, you are welcome here. This is what the perplexed and the traumatized need to hear. Connection, not alienation.

BE A FRIEND

Adopting a welcoming tone comes automatically if you picture the reader as a living, breathing, nonmathematical friend of yours. Rather than writing for a generic "intelligent reader," I imagined a real person when I wrote for the *New York Times*. It felt right to open the series by mentioning him, to establish an informal, affectionate tone and also to hint at the ideal reader I had in mind:

> I have a friend who gets a tremendous kick out of science, even though he's an artist. Whenever we get together all he wants to do is chat about the latest thing in evolution or quantum mechanics. But when it comes to math, he feels at sea, and it saddens him. The strange symbols keep him out. He says he doesn't even know how to pronounce them.
>
> In fact, his alienation runs a lot deeper. He's not sure what mathematicians do all day, or what they mean when they say a proof is elegant. Sometimes we joke that I just should sit him down and teach him everything, starting with 1 + 1 = 2 and going as far as we can (Strogatz 2010, "From Fish to Infinity").

I found that when thinking about specific tactical decisions in my writing, this orientation — treating the reader as a friend — always suggested what to do. For instance, it nudged me to make the following choices:

> 1) Keep algebraic manipulations to a minimum. My artist friend panics when the math gets too symbolic. The same is true for most of the perplexed and the traumatized. They get turned off by equations and shut down emotionally. It's much better, when possible, to recast the same mathematical idea pictorially.

2) Likewise, avoid sophisticated math symbols. Since most of the target readers won't know how to pronounce them, they won't be able to sound them out in their heads, which will tempt them to stop reading.

3) Don't number the diagrams. That gives them a textbook feel, another turnoff. And don't automatically place them at the top or bottom of the page (contrary to what most publishers would do by default). Instead, insist that the diagrams be placed in the text, surrounded by the words they illustrate. This is a friendly gesture; it saves the reader the trouble of hunting around for the diagram. In the same spirit, I asked my artist, Margy Nelson, to draw the diagrams in a cartoonish style. The hope was that the levity would refresh the reader when the going got tough.

Three Heroes

The strategies I've described here are all devices to help an outsider feel welcome. Three superb science writers — Richard Feynman, Stephen Jay Gould, and Lewis Thomas — approached this issue with exceptional flair. They took subjects that many readers would find forbidding, such as the edifice of modern physics, the vagaries of evolution, and the marvels of biology, and opened the door for everyone.

RICHARD FEYNMAN

What you notice first about Feynman is his voice. He's conversational, direct, and funny — always plain-spoken, but sometimes surprisingly lyrical. He comes across as a rascal: a playful, mischievous Brooklyn wise guy.

In his celebrated three-volume set of textbooks, *The Feynman Lectures on Physics*, here's how he opens his chapter on the principle of least action, one of the deepest ideas in all of physics:

"When I was in high school, my physics teacher — whose name was Mr. Bader — called me down one day after physics class and said, 'You look bored; I want to tell you something interesting.' Then he told me something which I found absolutely fascinating, and have, since then, always found fascinating. Every time the subject comes up, I work on it. In fact, when I began to prepare this lecture I found myself making more analyses on the thing. Instead of worrying about the lecture, I got involved in a new problem. The subject is this — the principle of least action" (1964, 2:19-1).

With his conversational style, he seems to be saying that physics is hard enough as it is — there's no need to make it harder by using fancy language or by putting on the formal airs of a textbook writer.

And he revels in telling the truth, especially about what remains unknown. For example, in another chapter he prefaces a discussion of thunderstorms by stressing how little we know about this commonplace phenomenon: "What is going on inside a thunderstorm? We will describe this insofar as it is known. As we get into this marvelous phenomenon of real nature — instead of the idealized spheres of perfect conductors inside of other spheres that we can solve so neatly — we discover that we don't know very much. Yet it is really quite exciting. Anyone who has been in a thunderstorm has enjoyed it, or has been frightened, or at least has had some emotion. And in those places in nature where we get an emotion, we find that there is generally a corresponding complexity and mystery about it. It is not going to be possible to describe exactly how a thunderstorm works, because we do not yet know very much. But we will try to describe a little bit about what happens" (1964, 2:9-5).

Any student reading this feels reassured. Not only is it okay not to know something, but it's exciting, because that's where new science is made, on the border between the known and the unknown. Feynman, one of the greatest physicists of the twentieth century, takes you there as your personal tour guide.

I had Feynman in mind when I wrote about calculus for the *New York Times* series. Knowing that many readers would quake at the thought of calculus as the Mount Everest of math, I tried to disarm their fears without dismissing them by casting my dad in the role of everyman and by mimicking Feynman's affable style:

> Long before I knew what calculus was, I sensed there was something special about it. My dad had spoken about it in reverential tones. He hadn't been able to go to college, being a child of the Depression, but somewhere along the line, maybe during his time in the South Pacific repairing B-24 bomber engines, he'd gotten a feel for what calculus could do. Imagine a mechanically controlled bank of anti-aircraft guns automatically firing at an incoming fighter plane. Calculus, he supposed, could be used to tell the guns where to aim.
>
> Every year about a million American students take calculus. But far fewer really understand what the subject is about or could tell you why they were learning it. It's not their fault. There are so many techniques to master and so many new ideas to absorb that the overall framework is easy to miss.
>
> Calculus is the mathematics of change. It describes everything from the spread of epidemics to the zigs and zags of a well-thrown curveball. The subject is gargantuan — and so are its textbooks. Many exceed 1,000 pages and work nicely as doorstops.
>
> But within that bulk you'll find two ideas shining through. All the rest, as Rabbi Hillel said of the Golden Rule, is just commentary. Those two ideas are the "derivative" and the "integral." Each dominates its own half of the subject, named in their honor as differential and integral calculus.

Roughly speaking, the derivative tells you how fast something is changing; the integral tells you how much it's accumulating. They were born in separate times and places: integrals, in Greece around 250 B.C.; derivatives, in England and Germany in the mid-1600s. Yet in a twist straight out of a Dickens novel, they've turned out to be blood relatives — though it took almost two millennia to see the family resemblance. (2010, "Change We Can Believe In")

The references to Dickens and Hillel were meant to signal that all are welcome here, including those with backgrounds in the humanities; those who found calculus bewildering the first time around; and those who, like my dad, never studied calculus at all.

But what I find about most inspiring in Feynman's writing, and what I tried to emulate in my own work, is his knack for delivering "Aha!" moments. His explanations, though phrased colloquially, are impeccable. They go straight to the heart of the matter. On almost any topic in any branch of physics, you will not find a more elegant and satisfying explanation than the one Feynman offers. He is the master of illumination.

STEPHEN JAY GOULD

In contrast to Feynman, Gould is the master of connections. Whereas Feynman lives and breathes for physics and physics alone, Gould links his subject — evolution — to the rest of existence in glorious detail. His essays range over science; history; philosophy; politics; architecture; and all parts of culture, high and low.

Two of his most famous essays draw on principles of evolutionary biology to explain why there are no longer any 0.400 hitters in baseball and why Mickey Mouse's facial features became progressively less ratlike and more adorably infantile (big eyes, big head, rounded features) during his first fifty years. In other pieces he explains why large animals have relatively thick leg bones, how insects walk up walls, why toddlers aren't hurt when they fall down, why medieval churches changed shape as they got larger, and how the creators of science fiction and horror movies embarrass themselves by overlooking these principles of size and scale when they depict giant ants or tiny people.

One of Gould's signature moves is to hook you with something light and unthreatening — a word, a story, a joke — to ease you into something sophisticated, the real subject of the piece. For instance, in his essay "Senseless Signs of History" he introduces a subtle idea in evolutionary biology, that "oddities in current terms are the signs of history," by coming in from the side:

> Words provide clues about their history when etymology does *not* match current meaning. Thus, we suspect that emoluments were once fees paid to the local miller (from the Latin *molere*, to grind), while disasters must have been blamed upon evil stars.
>
> Evolutionists have always viewed linguistic change as a fertile field for meaningful analogies. Charles Darwin, advocating an evolutionary interpretation for such vestigial structures as the human appendix and the embryonic teeth of whalebone whales, wrote: "Rudimentary organs may be compared with the letters in a word, still retained in the spelling, but [that] become useless in the pronunciation, but which serve as a clue in seeking for its derivation." Both organisms and languages evolve.
>
> This essay masquerades behind a list of curious facts, but it is really an abstract discourse on method — or, rather, on a particular method widely used but little appreciated by scientists. . . .
>
> Darwin reasoned, if organisms have a history, then ancestral stages should leave *remnants* behind. Remnants of the past that don't make sense in present terms — the useless, the odd, the pecu-

liar, the incongruous — are the signs of history. They supply proof that the world was not made in its present form. When history perfects, it covers its own tracks. (Gould 1980, 27–29)

I tried a similar sideways approach in the opening paragraphs of my column about group theory:

> My wife and I have different sleeping styles — and our mattress shows it. She hoards the pillows, thrashes around all night long, and barely dents the mattress, while I lie on my back, mummy-like, molding a cavernous depression into my side of the bed.
>
> Bed manufacturers recommend flipping your mattress periodically, probably with people like me in mind. But what's the best system? How exactly are you supposed to flip it to get the most even wear out of it?
>
> Brian Hayes explores this problem in the title essay of his recent book, "Group Theory in the Bedroom." Double entendres aside, the "group" in question here is a collection of mathematical actions — all the possible ways you could flip, rotate or overturn the mattress so that it still fits neatly on the bed frame.
>
> By looking into mattress math in some detail, I hope to give you a feeling for group theory more generally. It's one of the most versatile parts of mathematics. It underlies everything from the choreography of contra dancing and the fundamental laws of particle physics, to the mosaics of the Alhambra. (2010, "Group Think")

Unlike Feynman, however, Gould does not talk to you. He lectures at you. I never feel that he's my friend, and I wouldn't want to be stuck with him on a long car ride.

LEWIS THOMAS

My dream companion would be Thomas. He's funny and sunny, the most amiable science writer I've ever read. It's not that he doesn't see the world as it is, warts and all. It's that for him, even the warts are wonderful:

> Warts are wonderful structures. They can appear overnight on any part of the skin, like mushrooms on a damp lawn, full grown and splendid in the complexity of their architecture. Viewed in stained sections under a microscope, they are the most specialized of cellular arrangements, constructed as though for a purpose. They sit there like herded mounds of dense, impenetrable horn, impregnable, designed for defense against the world outside....
>
> The strangest thing about warts is that they tend to go away. Fully grown, nothing in the body has so much the look of toughness and permanence as a wart, and yet, inexplicably and often very abruptly, they come to the end of their lives and vanish without a trace.
>
> And they can be made to go away by something that can only be called thinking, or something like thinking. This is a special property of warts which is absolutely astonishing, more of a surprise than cloning or recombinant DNA or endorphin or acupuncture or anything else currently attracting attention in the press. It is one of the great mystifications of science: warts can be ordered off the skin by hypnotic suggestion. (1980, 61)

This is the delight of Lewis Thomas. He sees the universe in a grain of sand or, in his case, in a wart.

He's also, for my money, the best stylist of all science writers. His sentences have a lilt and a rhythm and a snap to them. So do his words and his paragraphs. He's graceful at every scale, from punctuation to paragraph.

Read this passage out loud to hear what I mean:

> You start out as a single cell derived from the coupling of a sperm and an egg, this divides into two, then four, then eight,

and so on, and at a certain stage there emerges a single cell which will have as all its progeny the human brain. The mere existence of that cell should be one of the great astonishments of the earth. People ought to be walking around all day, all through their waking hours, calling to each other in endless wonderment, talking of nothing except that cell. It is an unbelievable thing, and yet there it is, popping neatly into its place amid the jumbled cells of every one of the several billion human embryos around the planet, just as if it were the easiest thing in the world to do. (1980, 130–31)

Or this:

The capacity to blunder slightly is the real marvel of DNA. Without this special attribute, we would still be anaerobic bacteria and there would be no music. Viewed individually, one by one, each of the mutations that have brought us along represents a random, totally spontaneous accident, but it is no accident at all that mutations occur; the molecule of DNA was ordained from the beginning to make small mistakes.

If we had been doing it, we would have found some way to correct this, and evolution would have been stopped in its tracks. Imagine the consternation of human scientists, successfully engaged in the letter-perfect replication of prokaryotes, non-nucleated cells like bacteria, when nucleated cells suddenly turned up. Think of the agitated commissions assembled to explain the scandalous proliferation of trilobites all over the place, the mass firings, the withdrawal of tenure. (1980, 23)

I especially love his surprising juxtapositions. "The strangest thing about warts is that they tend to go away." *That's* the strangest thing?

Sometimes the surprises come in staccato bursts, like a prize-fighter throwing a combination: "The capacity to blunder slightly is the real marvel of DNA. Without this special attribute, we would still be anaerobic bacteria and there would be no music." Bang, bang, bang, boom!

I was hoping to achieve a similar effect, in muted form, in this opening to a piece about differential geometry: "The most familiar ideas of geometry were inspired by an ancient vision — a vision of the world as flat. From parallel lines that never meet, to the Pythagorean theorem discussed in last week's column, these are eternal truths about an imaginary place, the two-dimensional landscape of plane geometry" (2010, "Think Globally").

Saying something nice about flat-earth thinking and juxtaposing eternal truths and imaginary places were my attempts (pale as they may have been) to play with the reader's expectations in the manner of Lewis Thomas.

Although Feynman, Gould, and Thomas use different tactics, it seems to me that they've all converged on the same secret, the key to communicating difficult technical subjects to the masses. Clear writing? Sure. Beautiful explanations? Of course. But none of that is enough.

The real secret is empathy. These heroes of science writing help us love the questions they're asking. They do whatever it takes to make us feel at home in a strange land.

Epilogue

My *New York Times* series, "The Elements of Math," debuted on January 31, 2010. The response from readers far surpassed what I could have dreamed of. For fifteen straight weeks, the columns attracted hundreds of comments and climbed the list of most e-mailed articles, occasionally reaching the top. Here are a few sample reactions to the first column:

- Thank you thank you thank you! I've been waiting for you all my adult life. I've always felt I am colour-blinded for math; perhaps this time around I'll finally be able to make friends with it.
- We, the innumerate, thank you.
- Great! I am a math phobic, an artist, but very curious to learn again in a new way. I am excited!
- This is exciting! I'm an English teacher, but also a science enthusiast. I've always, however, been hobbled by my poor math skills. What a testament to the survival of intellect, that a column about mathematics could generate buzz and (at this writing) almost 500 positive and encouraging comments. I look forward to this. Thank you.

My favorite reaction, though, came from my neighbor Lauren, a photographer. She said that reading my series made her *want* to like math.

Not quite what I was shooting for, but hey, it's a start.

REFERENCES

Feynman, Richard P., Robert B. Leighton, and Matthew Sands. 1964. *The Feynman Lectures on Physics.* 3 vols. Boston: Addison-Wesley.

Gould, Stephen Jay. 1980. *The Panda's Thumb: More Reflections in Natural History.* New York: W. W. Norton.

Strogatz, Steven. 2010. "The Elements of Math." *New York Times.* http://topics.nytimes.com/top/opinion/series/steven_strogatz_on_the_elements_of_math/index.html. (The individual columns appeared in slightly modified form in Steven Strogatz, 2012, *The Joy of x: A Guided Tour of Math, from One to Infinity* [London: Houghton Mifflin Harcourt]).

Thomas, Lewis. 1980. *The Medusa and the Snail: More Notes of a Biology Watcher.* New York: Bantam.

KATHLEEN BLAKE YANCEY

two Notes toward a Theory of Writing for the Public

My title promises notes toward a theory of writing for the public. The following questions can set the stage: Why do we write for the public, and why might we?[1] And in doing so, how do we write? What are the contexts and the rhetorical strategies that would be compelling to those who are not, apparently, us?

In asking these questions, I'm assuming that there is a we and that there is a public, although clearly, there are numerous we's, plural publics.[2] Still, at least in the United States (and likely elsewhere), those in the academy have often taken up the cause of explaining their research to the public: that's one reason to write. We know more about astronomy because of Carl Sagan, about medicine because of Atul Gawande, about black culture because of Henry Louis Gates, Jr., about presidential rhetoric because of Kathleen Jamieson.

Interestingly, in writing studies we have taken a somewhat different approach to writing for the public than have the scholars above. Their impulse seems to be to explain — indeed, to translate — their research so that members of the public might understand, while in writing studies we seem to want to share our research largely for the sake of advocacy: to persuade. Given that writing studies is, in Joe Harris's well-known formulation, a "teaching subject," perhaps it's not surprising that we want the public both to understand and to act. More specifically, we want the public to understand what it's like to teach writing, what such teaching involves as a material matter, and what help students need. Indeed, we want the public to understand what writing is — not grammar, not editing, but rhetorical suasion, often for the public good. Given this understanding, the public will, we hope, provide more support and contribute to better learning conditions for our students as well as better teaching conditions for our colleagues and ourselves. Seen in this light, Mike Rose's award-winning *Lives on the Boundary*, a narrative account of his struggles and ultimate achievement in school, is at least as much argument as it is narrative about the institution of school, about how school categorizes, frustrates, and too often fails students. Other examples of writing studies' faculty members' going public, however, are located outside of narrative and inside of argument — and specifically a less subtle, more agonistic argument. Les Perelman's critique of the recently introduced sat writing test (Wertheimer 2005), for example, which was made public at nearly the same moment as the National Council of Teachers of English's report on "The Impact of the sat and act Timed Writing Tests" (2005), is a classic example. Perelman's intent was twofold: to help the public understand how diminished the sat's construct of writing was, and to rally members of the public — parents, teachers, and students — to pressure the College Board to abandon such a measure, or to encourage parents and students to opt out of it.[3]

In sum, as I pointed out in "Connecting with Our Publics" (2010), our motive in writing studies for writing to the public seems, in Lloyd Bitzer's terms, to identify an exigence that we want to address and resolve.[4] Indeed, with the goal of designing such a situation, I proposed a heuristic that could help us craft messages for the public:

- What's the exigence?
- What does the research show?

- How much space is there in the national or local discourse for this issue? Put differently, how salient is the exigence, and for which publics?
- What's the goal or aspirational outcome?
- Who else is interested? Are there expected educational partners, or are others already engaged in ways that can be tapped?
- Which media others can be engaged (institutional press, local or national reporters)?
- How can attention (think of Richard Lanham's economy of attention) be sustained and/or increased?
- Given possible outcomes, what are follow-up activities?

But in retrospect, a(nother) question: Is this the only way, or even the best way, to write to the public?

* * *

Writing studies is a culture; scholars in other cultures behave differently. All researchers in math, for example, may not talk to the public, but one of their major scholarly bodies, the American Mathematical Society (AMS), does so routinely. In its print publications and on its website, it includes posters in the Mathematical Moments series, which is specifically designed to explain math to the public. In the language of the AMS (n.d.), the Mathematical Moments program "promotes appreciation and understanding of the role mathematics plays in science, nature, technology, and human culture" (figure 2.1). Put differently, these posters are produced not to persuade members of the public that they should act, but rather to share with them the interesting ways that math shapes our everyday existence. In that sense, perhaps the key word here isn't "understanding," but rather "appreciation."

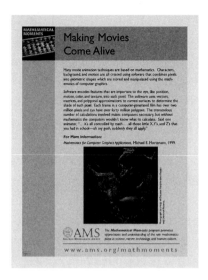

FIGURE 2.1 American Mathematical Society, "Making Movies Come Alive," 2000. Mathematical Moments.

Which makes me wonder: How do these intents differ, and how might each influence our writing for the public?

* * *

One mathematician who has taken up writing for the public and whose twofold intent is to foster both understanding and appreciation is, of course, Steven Strogatz, whose essay is included in this volume. Reflecting on his own writing for the public, Strogatz notes three challenges entailed in writing about math (and other technical disciplines) for the public: the subject is "inherently abstract," is expressed through "strange symbols and jargon," and can prompt "phobia and anxiety." As Strogatz says, "you'd think we were discussing spiders," and — we might note — discussing them though in foreign symbols and probably to someone who'd never seen them. Toward the end of his essay, Strogatz points to features that he finds make writing for the public compelling: "The real secret is empathy." In their writing, Richard Feynman, Stephen Jay Gould, and Lewis Thomas "help us love the questions they're asking. They do whatever it takes to make us feel at home in a strange land." From Strogatz's perspective, in employing empathy — "help[ing] us love the questions they're asking" — writers invite the public into the writer's world: through empathy and questions, we readers become not strangers in a new land, but "at home."

In Strogatz's own writing, we see other rhetorical strategies that are examples of how academics and scholars might write to the public, two of which are particularly important. First, Strogatz writes about commonplace everyday experiences to draw readers in, while emphasizing the contribution that math can make to our understanding. In one column for the *New York Times*, for example, Strogatz takes up the issue of how one should flip a mattress on a bed, leading into it by contrasting the ways that he and his wife sleep, which of course is another everyday experience:

> My wife and I have different sleeping styles — and our mattress shows it. She hoards the pillows, thrashes around all night long, and barely dents the mattress, while I lie on my back, mummy-like, molding a cavernous depression into my side of the bed.
>
> Bed manufacturers recommend flipping your mattress periodically, probably with people like me in mind. But what's the best system? How exactly are you supposed to flip it to get the most even wear out of it?

It turns out that determining how we should flip our mattresses, which Strogatz calls "mattress math" (figure 2.2), is related — who knew? — to something called "group theory," which is "one of the most versatile parts of mathematics. It underlies everything from the choreography of contra dancing and the fundamental laws

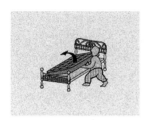

FIGURE 2.2 Margaret
Nelson, "Mattress Math,"
in Steven Strogatz, "Group
Think," *New York Times*,
May 2, 2010.

of particle physics, to the mosaics of the Alhambra." Here, then,
we see Strogatz at work: beginning the theory by situating it in
a domestic sphere that many people, at least in the West, have
experienced, then linking it to a mathematical interpretation
that Strogatz calls "mattress math," a clever mnemonic device
to help us remember what the theory is explaining. In addition,
he links this theory to other experiences that we might have encountered, including dancing and art, a wide range for a short list
of experiences. Not least important, he uses images, too, so those
who think visually have a more hospitable point of reference.
In other columns, Strogatz includes videos of cultural icons like
Sesame Street characters and basketball great Michael Jordan
that, again, show the everyday nature of the kinds of problems
that math helps us address. In sum, through providing a variety
of material — small narratives, explanations in word and numbers,
images and graphs, videos, cultural icons, and references to other
materials and links — Strogatz creates multiple points of entry
into each column and thus makes it more available to many. We
enter through the experience most familiar to us and through the
medium — print, image, or video — that we prefer.

A second strategy that Strogatz employs is punning, which we
see in the title of another column, this one addressing probability:
"Chances Are" (2010). "Have you ever had," he asks, "that anxiety dream where you suddenly realize you have to take the final
exam in some course you've never attended? For professors, it

works the other way around — you dream you're giving a lecture for a class you know nothing about." In this case, what he knows "nothing about" is probability theory, and he compares the feeling of explaining it to the thrill of a carnival ride: "That's what it's like for me whenever I teach probability theory. It was never part of my own education, so having to lecture about it now is scary and fun, in an amusement park, thrill-house sort of way." He proceeds to explain it to us anyway. The title of this column, "Chances Are," is defined in part through the image of two dice, which tells us right away one way to interpret it. But when I read the title, I heard Johnny Mathis singing "Chances Are," one of my favorites; in my mind's eye, I saw the promotional flyer for the movie *Chances Are*, featuring Cybill Shepherd. Here, then, Strogatz's provision of multiple points of entry through a collective cultural memory is less direct but every bit as powerful.

* * *

But perhaps when scholars in writing studies write for the public they do more than advocate and persuade; perhaps we too want the public to understand and appreciate. Upon reflection, I see that we have designed two other ways of writing for the public, one fairly conventional for some disciplines but new for us, the second a more crowd-sourced approach that is less writing for the public than writing with it. The first approach is represented in the poster pages hosted by the journal *College Composition and Communication*. Inspired in part by the Mathematical Moments series and in part by the posters published in the *Journal of the American Medical Association*, which explain various illnesses, conditions, and syndromes to the public, each *College Composition and Communication* poster page highlights a key concept in writing studies — one on rhetorical situation, for example, and another on composing. Designed for the public, each page

Writing across the Curriculum/Writing in the Disciplines

Writing across the Curriculum

Definition

Writing takes place in a community, and on college campuses we have many kinds of community, which tend to be organized into programs, departments, fields, or disciplines. Each of these includes its own writing processes as well as its own genres. Given this situation, it's impossible for any writing course—including first-year composition—to prepare students for all the writing they will need to do, and do well, in college. Thus, it wasn't surprising that in the 1960s and 1970s an educational effort called Writing across the Curriculum developed. Writing across the Curriculum—or WAC, as it's often called now—emphasizes the role that writing can play in learning, whether it's keeping a journal, annotating a text, making field notes, or reflecting on what we have learned. Later, programs more targeted to writing *inside* specific disciplines have developed. Writing in the Disciplines—or WID—helps students behave as apprentice writers in that discipline, be it civil engineering, sociology, or dance.

Importance to the Field

Many colleges and universities offer WAC, WID, or WAC/WID programs supporting students' development in writing. Even institutions that don't offer a formal program, however, often include writing to learn activities as well as support for writing inside the discipline. And we know that this kind of progression is critical for students' writing development.

Resources

Carter, Michael. "Ways of Knowing, Doing, and Writing in the Disciplines." *College Composition and Communication* 58.3 (2007): 385–418. Print.

Herrington, Anne, and Charles Moran, eds. *Genre across the Curriculum.* Logan: Utah State UP, 2005. Print.

McLeod, Susan H., Eric Miraglia, Margot Soven, and Christopher Thaiss. *WAC for the New Millennium: Strategies for Continuing Writing across the Curriculum Programs.* Urbana: NCTE, 2001. Print. Available at http://wac.colostate.edu/books/millennium/

Reiss, Donna, Dickie Selfe, and Art Young, eds. *Electronic Communication across the Curriculum.* Urbana: NCTE, 1998. Print.

Russell, David R. *Writing in the Academic Disciplines: A Curricular History.* 2nd ed. Carbondale: Southern Illinois UP, 2002. Print.

Thaiss, Chris, and Tara Porter. "The State of WAC/WID in 2010: Methods and Results of the U.S. Survey of the International WAC/WID Mapping Project." *College Composition and Communication* 61.3 (2010): 534–70. Print.

CCC
College Composition and Communication

FIGURE 2.3

Kathleen Yancey, "Writing Across the Curriculum/Writing in the Disciplines," 2013. *College Composition and Communication* 64, no. 3: 580.

DALH Home
Login

Digital Archive of Literacy Narratives

Welcome! The Digital Archives of Literacy Narratives (DALN) is a publicly available archive of personal literacy narratives in a variety of formats (text, video, audio) that together provide a historical record of the literacy practices and values of contributors, as those practices and values change.

The DALN invites people of all ages, races, communities, backgrounds, and interests to contribute stories about how — and in what circumstances — they read, write, and compose meaning, and how they learned to do so (or helped others learn). We welcome personal narratives about reading and composing all kinds of texts, both formal and informal: diaries, blogs, poetry, music and musical lyrics, fan zines, school papers, videos, sermons, gaming profiles, speeches, chatroom exchanges, text messages, letters, stories, photographs, etc. We also invite contributors to supplement their narratives with samples of their own writing (papers, letters, zines, speeches, etc.) and compositions (music, photographs, videos, sound recordings, etc.).

If you would like more detailed information about creating a literacy narrative and contributing it to the DALN, please visit our resources and help pages .

To submit your literacy narrative, you must first register with the DALN, a simple process that requires only a valid e-mail address. Once you have registered, you can login and submit a narrative .

Register | **Login** | **Submit a Narrative** | **Consult Resources** | **View Contributing Partners**
Why do we ask you to register?

FIGURE 2.4

Digital Archive of Literacy Narratives home page.

is divided into three areas: definition, importance to the field, and resources (figure 2.3). The hope is that the posters will explain writing as we currently understand and teach it. A second approach to connecting with the public is the Digital Archive of Literacy Narratives, an archive of stories about how we have learned to read and write that everyone can contribute to and consult (figure 2.4). In engaging people in telling their stories and in archiving them, those of us in the field of writing studies, and more specifically Cynthia Selfe and her colleagues at Ohio State University, acknowledge the lived experience of all of us, academics and members of the public. Because of its participatory nature, this approach may be especially persuasive.

I began this chapter by asking questions about why and how we write to the public: *Why do we write for the public, and why might we? And in doing so, how do we write? What are the contexts and the rhetorical strategies that would be compelling to those who are not, apparently, us?* In thinking about these questions, what seems apparent is that we write to the public because we have something to share, and across the disciplines — from math and medicine to composition — what we all most want to share is located in our own humanity.

That, at least, is a good place for all of us to begin.

NOTES

1. Writing for the public is different from engaging the public, as Michael Robinson explains in a response to Seth Kahn:

> The In These Times article you linked to seems to me a prime example of engaging the public. The teacher's union there didn't just come in with an agenda and present that to parents. They have gone out, visited homes, asked for and listened to what the parents are saying about what they need. The[y] didn't assume that they already knew how parents viewed them or what they wanted for their kids. That's dialogue; that's engagement.

What interested me about the topic of this thread is the concept of the need to listen. For me politically, rhetorically, and more importantly, in the simple attempt to understand what's happening, listening must precede and accompany action. It seems that some folks feel that they've done enough listening to know what we should be doing right now. But there are others of us who don't feel that way, who want to hear more and connect more, not because we don't want to act but because we wonder about the extent to which our failure to listen contributes to some of the problems we are facing. For those who want to focus on action, then by all means, act. But for my purposes, even beyond generating successful political power, I want to know more about what's happening. I want to understand what various public(s) think they are doing and why. I see value in that.

So does anyone besides me still want to talk about how to engage the public? (2013, n.p.)

2. For a discussion of the publics that composition scholars and teachers work with and toward, see Welch's recent review in *College Composition and Communication* (2012).

3. The SAT Writing Test no longer is administered, and it's fair to note that the number of schools that have gone test-optional continues to increase; though we can't prove causality, there is certainly a correlation between this writing for the public and the increase in this number.

4. Sometimes there are genuine exigences linked to the public interest in terms of fundamentals like survival. Such an exigence was created by the 1906 San Francisco earthquake, as Mary Miller of the San Francisco Exploratorium explains: "The 1906 earthquake did more than shake up northern California, it also jolted geologists into focusing on how and why faults break loose. It was the decisive action of a dedicated group of scientists that would make that violent 300-mile (480 km) rupture of the San Andreas Fault one of the most carefully studied and thoroughly documented earthquakes in the United States. The report that these pioneering geologists produced has become a bedrock of our current understanding of earthquake hazards and seismology and is widely admired as a model scientific study. Its vivid, clear prose, attention to scientific detail, thoroughness and accuracy, and numerous photographs,

maps, and diagrams make it a relevant and fascinating read to this day" (n.d.).

REFERENCES

American Mathematical Society. n.d. Mathematical Moments. http://www.ams.org/samplings/mathmoments/browsemoments?cat=all.

Bitzer, Lloyd. 1968. "The Rhetorical Situation." *Philosophy and Rhetoric* 1, no. 1: 1–14.

Harris, Joseph. 2012. *A Teaching Subject: Composition since 1966*. New ed. Logan: Utah State University Press.

Miller, Mary Kay. n.d. "Science from the Ashes." Exploratorium. http://www.exploratorium.edu/faultline/great/science.html.

National Council of Teachers of English. 2005. "The Impact of the SAT and ACT Timed Writing Tests." April. http://www.ncte.org/library /NCTEFiles/Resources/Positions/SAT-ACT-tf-report.pdf.

Robinson, Michael. 2013. "Re: Engaging with the General Public." Unpublished manuscript.

Rose, Mike. 2005. *Lives on the Boundary*. New ed. New York: Penguin.

Strogatz, Steven. 2010. "The Elements of Math." *New York Times*. http://topics.nytimes.com/top/opinion/series/steven_strogatz_on _the_elements_of_math/index.html. (The individual columns appeared in slightly modified form in Steven Strogatz, 2012, *The Joy of x: A Guided Tour of Math, from One to Infinity* [London: Houghton Mifflin Harcourt]).

Welch, Nancy. 2012. "The Point Is to Change It: Problems and Prospects for Public Rhetors." *College Composition and Communication* 63, no. 4: 699–714.

Wertheimer, Linda. 2005. "MIT Professor Finds Fault with SAT Essay." National Public Radio, May 7. http://www.npr.org/templates/story /story.php?storyId=4634566.

Yancey, Kathleen. 2010. "Connecting with Our Publics: Some Observations." Paper presented at the annual Conference on College Composition and Communication, Louisville, KY, March 18.

DANIEL ROCKMORE

three Writing in the Sciences

When I try to think carefully about the challenges that are particular to writing in the sciences, I seem to continually circle back to the belief that, at their core, they are those that generally confront any specialist working to communicate his or her "disciplinary" understandings to a broader audience. I use quotation marks because although the subject at hand — that of "writing in the disciplines" — has an academic genesis, I see this as a particular case of a much more general question: What are the challenges inherent in trying to communicate somewhat specialized, even personal, knowledge to others who necessarily have a knowledge base different from your own? Framed in this way, it is nothing less than the basic challenge of communication tackled by any person who writes for other people, independent of whether he or she wishes to communicate ideas in the sciences, humanities, social sciences, business, medicine, sports, or other field. So although it may be of special interest in the academy, where the written communication of ideas — even in the digital, but not quite postwriting, age — still underlies the activities of the marketplace, it is worth recognizing that its relevance surely extends beyond the academy.

Let me now bring the conversation back to my home base of the sciences, momentarily ignoring the diversity among the sciences to first consider the general activity of writing in the sciences. To begin, there are many different kinds of writing in the sciences. Largely, they are distinguished by their target audiences, which expand out from a core of specialists to the broader disciplinary community, on through an even broader community of scientists, and then again through something of a hierarchy that eventually can encompass the entire literate world. This hierarchy of audience is reflected in something of a reverse hierarchy of language: as the audience expands, the technical vocabulary recedes. Precision may soften to metaphor.

Regardless of audience, the usual goal of writing in the sciences is one of clarity — that is, the clear communication of a scientific idea. To that end, I believe that ultimately clarity is in the eye of the reader. This strikes me as the most important thing to remember for any writer trying to communicate scientific ideas: attend to your audience. In short, practice selfless or empathetic writing by trying to put yourself in the mind of your intended reader.

When writing for the relatively tiny audience of our own specialties, such writerly selflessness is effectively second nature due to the shared backgrounds and language of the specialized scientific community. It's also often assisted (or perhaps hamstrung!) by the codified nature of most writing intended for publication in a journal (some journals even specify the format and style of the work). However, as soon as we start to stray outside of our specialties, empathy requires vigilance — it is easy to forget what it is that the reader might not know. Again, this goes on at multiple levels. It can happen within a discipline (for example, in mathematics when the number theorist writes for the topologist) as easily as across scientific disciplines (for example, when the mathematician writes for the biologist). Finally, a scientist attempting to reach an entirely different academic division (such as the mathematician writing for the art historian or sociologist) must surely be the most conscientious. The chasm between C. P. Snow's famous two cultures is both wide and deep.

Moving beyond the academy, the challenges are surely the greatest when the working scientist tries to enter the world of popular science writing, an experience that for many of us can turn that odd phrase into something of an oxymoron. In this arena, selfless writing can feel like a torturous balancing act, requiring us to navigate as it were between the Scylla of the broad public's general lack of familiarity with the subject matter and the Charybdis of disdain of other members of one's professional community, who can be quick to take issue with either a dumbing down of an idea or the smoothing of a technical subtlety in the service of expository necessities. The latter of these is a real danger, so much so that many a junior faculty member is encouraged to avoid expository work before earning tenure. Although the tide may be turning, communication with the public generally (and sadly) is not yet valued as highly as research publication, even regardless of venue. As an aside, one unfortunate artifact of this is the working scientist's general invisibility in the public sphere. To this end, the only advice I can give about popular science writing to those who might consider undertaking it is to remind them that this kind of science writing — and, more generally, science communication — is extraordinarily important. Ultimately, the health of the sciences as a profession and (in our increasingly science- and technology-dependent society) the level of public discourse depend on the public's knowing what we do.

Implicit in popular science writing is a tension between accessibility and detail, the latter of which is often conflated with truth. Einstein is known for saying that in mathematical models "everything should be made as simple as possible, but not simpler." This strikes me as the technical analogue of the advice that a friend who has made his own reasonably successful forays into exposition gave me: "Good science writing is telling the truth, but not the whole truth." When writing for the general public, keep in mind the main truth that you are trying to communicate. If the caveats start to overwhelm the main idea, then perhaps that main idea isn't the correct distillation. That said, none of this means that writing has to dumb science down. In fact, the best science writing probably pushes its audience a bit. After all, such writing is intended to communicate new information to its readers, but accomplishing this necessarily means meeting them on their own terms (by providing simple examples in common language and using familiar analogies) and not overwhelming readers with too much information.

I'd like to close with a few remarks that are particular to writing for the public about my own field, mathematics. The communication of mathematics has some very special challenges, largely related to the fact that although in other sciences (and we'll neglect for the moment the question of whether or not mathematics should be lumped in with the sciences) the subjects of interest are embodied in tangible entities (for example, brains, stars, atoms, frogs, cells, and people), mathematics often concerns itself with Platonic products of pure thought — numbers, geometries, topologies, and the like, most of which are expressed in an extraordinary shorthand of symbolic notation. Furthermore, a good deal of mathematics is about plumbing the depths of the relationships between these symbols — not all, but a good deal. In a real sense, the mathematics that has direct referents in the real world and experiential analogues is truly the tip of the iceberg of the subject. Another challenge derives from the unhappy truth that a large fraction of the general public has little familiarity with mathematics and, for many people in that fraction, less than happy associations with it. There is an old and perhaps legendary maxim in the publishing world that every equation in a written work cuts your audience in half. That's a pretty daunting statement for those of us whose work is about equations! That said, I do believe that working to find a way to bring those symbols and ideas to life for people who stopped thinking about mathematics some time ago, but who find themselves intrigued by what they might have missed, is a lot like working on a good problem: it's a tractable puzzle that, with effort, brings understanding and deep satisfaction.

part 2 Social Sciences

DAVID MCCULLOUGH

four The Good, Hard Work of Writing Well

I'm always glad to be back here at Dartmouth. I love Dartmouth. I think it's one of the choice places in all our country.

We are here to address the important topic of writing. Very much needs to be done about the teaching of writing at a time when skill with our language seems so obviously in decline in so many quarters — when so many college graduates, for example, seem incapable of writing a presentable letter or report.

* * *

In California once, years ago, a high school student realized she had never been inside the local public library. She entered for the first time, looked around, and then at random picked a book off a shelf. She read the first page and decided she had to read that book. She was told at the desk she could not take the book out until she had a library card and could not get a card immediately. She went to a bookstore. The store didn't have it. So she returned to the library and stole the book.

Later in life she became the head of the English department at one of our major universities. She had read the first page of the novel *The Woman of Andros*, by Thornton Wilder. The book — Wilder's way of writing — changed her life.

I knew Thornton Wilder when I was a student at Yale. He was a major presence and an inspiration. So were John O'Hara; Richard

This piece was originally delivered as a lecture without notes.

Flint in geology; Vincent Scully, the architecture historian; and the author John Hersey. All of us who were their students are forever indebted. These were people who set a high mark for those of us who wanted to write or be creative in a number of fields. There is no such thing as a self-made man or woman. We are all the result of teachers, parents, friends, rivals, and those we've come to know whom we've never met because we've come to know them in books, in poetry and drama. Life isn't long enough to appreciate the pure gold of just our literary heritage and all to be learned therein.

We speak a language that isn't ours. It's been handed down to us with a tradition of expression and power that is well worth a lifetime of study, and particularly for those for whom writing is a way of life. I love what I do. I love every day of it. Happiness — true happiness — is not to be found in vacations or the like. It's to be found in the love of learning and doing what you really want to get up and get to each day. And yes, happiness is to be found in writing, because, for one thing, writing focuses the brain like nothing else.

Writing is hard work, make no mistake, but that's what makes it so captivating. Writing is a chance to enlarge life. When I was in my twenties, I saw the Western author Harry Sinclair Drago one evening at a gathering of writers in New York. A friend said: "See that old fellow over there? He's written more than a hundred books!" I approached Mr. Drago and asked him how he did it. "Four pages a day," he said.

His point was clear: you learn to write by writing, just as you learn to paint by painting or to play the piano by playing the piano. As an old piano teacher liked to say to her students, "I hear all the notes, but I hear no music."

Write to make music. Don't just pound out notes. We are all trying to make music.

There is no one way to write. It's what works for you. Very often, you won't know what works for you until you've done those four pages a day maybe for four or five years.

It's when you begin writing that you begin to see how much more you need to know. There are so many people who have such interesting lives that have yet to be discovered and shared with others. Leads are everywhere. There's never going to be a shortage of ideas out there in the world. So share your ideas with others! Tell others what you're working on. You never know whence or from whom that "trunk in the attic full of historic treasures" will come.

Do research as you write, not just before you write. Do research from the beginning to the end — and then you might even want to keep researching after you're done.

Go where things happened and walk the walk. Go to the Kentucky coal town or the boulevards of Paris if that's what is needed. If you're writing about the jungles of Panama, go there. Remember the five senses. What was the smell in the air? How did the light fall? What were the sounds of early morning?

Charles Dickens's great admonition to writers was, "Make me see."

My wonderful old high school English teacher, Lowell Innes, used to say over and over, "Don't tell me. Show me."

Take drawing lessons. Try painting. It will teach you how to look at things as you never have. Learn to observe closely. *And then take time to think about it.*

And read a lot. Don't just read what others have written, read what they read too. This is particularly important when trying to understand or portray life in a time very different from our own. When the HBO producers asked me for advice about preparing the miniseries on John Adams, I told them: "Please don't let it become a costume pageant. Life then must be shown to be as difficult and often unpleasant as it truly was, and please don't violate the vocabulary of the eighteenth century." Writers ought not violate the vocabulary of other times any more than they should distort the facts.

One of the most obvious differences between writing history and fiction is the inability to create dialogue. When writing history, you can't invent what people said. You have to go find what they said — in letters, diaries, court testimony, and so forth. And there's plenty to be found. Writing history is like working on a detective case. And once on the case, you want to know more and more and more. Follow your curiosity. Our curiosity is what separates us from the cabbages. And curiosity, happily, is accelerative like gravity.

The job is to bring historical characters to life. Your subjects were real human beings, after all. Show their strengths, their failings. And remember you're writing about people who didn't know how things would turn out, any more than we do.

In a very real way there is no such thing as the past. And no one ever lived in the past. They were living in the present, *their* present, much as we do. History is human, let us remember. "When in the course of human events . . ." — the key word there is "human."

There is every chance to be as creative writing history as there is writing fiction. There are many stories too long untold, and no shortage of topics to pursue. Things often happen in real life that if you were to put them in a novel, people would say, "That's too unrealistic!" even though it was what actually happened. I would be very happy writing fiction. Real life, though, is so often so much more remarkable.

I'm not an expert. I don't ever want to be an expert. Experts supposedly have all the answers. I prefer having questions. If I knew all about the subject, I wouldn't want to write a book about it. I want the project to be a journey, an adventure.

I've never wanted to work by an outline. It would be like painting by the numbers.

I try to write the kind of book that I would like to read. When I was working on my history of the Brooklyn Bridge, I met a woman who thought the whole idea preposterous and told me so. "Who in the world would ever want to read a book about the Brooklyn Bridge?" she exclaimed. Well, the answer was, "I would."

When I talk with some of my academic friends about a project I'm working on, they will often ask about my theme. So I make something up. In reality, I have no idea what the theme is. That's one of the reasons I'm writing the book — to find out what the theme is. I've never undertaken a book on a subject I know all about. The great pull of a project is the thought of how much I'm going to learn.

I don't think one should write to tell people what you want them to think. I want readers to draw their own conclusions from the story I have to tell.

It's part of our human nature to want to know something about what happened before we appeared on the scene. "Once upon a time, long, long ago" are ever magic words. We've survived as a species for thousands of years by passing on what subsequent generations need to know about life through the vehicle of story. We need stories. We have an old, old story hunger, thank heaven.

* * *

And now, from my own experience, here is some practical advice about writing:

Don't fool around about beginning what you have to say. Don't sit tapping your foot for a paragraph or two. Get right on with it, get up and dance. But remember, beginnings *are* crucial! They set the direction and tone.

Let your characters speak for themselves as often as possible.

Write for the ear as well as the eye. Read what you've written aloud, or have someone read it to you. And listen closely. You'll hear mistakes you don't see.

Put what you've written on the shelf for a while and then read it again. Very often you'll see ways to make it better that had eluded you.

Rewrite, rewrite, and rewrite. When asked if I'm a writer, I think sometimes I should say, "No, I'm a rewriter."

People today seem always to want to work fast or faster. I want to go more slowly. That's one of the reasons I work on a typewriter. Now there's no one way to work, but going slowly works best for me. My children used to go to sleep at night to the familiar sound of the keys of my typewriter.

Read good writers, especially while working on a project. I crave the release that comes with reading a great novel or great poetry. Try reading geographically or across time. Read everything good that you can get your hands on. Read Penelope Lively and Billy Collins. Read the letters of Flannery O'Connor. Read the murder mysteries of Ruth Rendell. Reading good writers is one of the greatest pleasures in life, but it's also a professional necessity. You have to keep the mind in shape.

History should not ever be dull; it should never be made boring by boring teachers or boring writers. We are raising generations of young Americans who, by and large, are historically illiterate. And that has to change. There is no better way to understand who we are and why we are the way we are and where we may be heading than by reading history from the hands of good writers. I can't imagine a world without books. And that's where I will end my talk.

KEITH GILYARD

five Growing Writers

A Response to David McCullough

Before directly addressing the comments made by David Mc-
Cullough, I would like to gesture toward the 1966 Dartmouth
conference. Two of its participants, Wayne Booth and James
Britton, influenced me both through conversation and through
their work. A third attendee, Geoffrey Summerfield, became a
professor of mine. As I recall the tremendous guidance that he
provided, I can still imagine him quoting Roland Barthes to our
class: "One writes in order to be loved" (1972, 279). Barthes was
referring in that instance to the impossibility of written language's
capturing all of a person's thoughts and feelings on a specific occasion. Any rendition is only one of many that could have been
supplied relative to a set of experiences. Writing, in a large sense,
is organizing, filtering, and presenting for admiration. This observation relates to a statement by John Dixon in his report on
the 1966 Dartmouth gathering titled *Growth through English*: "In
ordering and composing situations that in some way symbolize life
as we know it, we bring order and composure to our inner selves.
When a pupil is steeped in language in operation we expect, as he
matures, a conceptualizing of his earlier awareness of language,
and with this perhaps new insights into himself (as a creator of
his own world)" (1967, 13). I would say the creator of *a* world, and
something that a *she* could also do. And I would emphasize the

*This piece was originally delivered as a response to David McCullough's
lecture at the 2012 Dartmouth Writing Summit.*

ideas of "own" and "inner self." We could spend hours discussing the relationship between inner self and language, which is a social instrument. However, the point I want to stress is that the conception of writing as an act to provide understanding — what Britton termed "shaping at the point of utterance" (1982, 110) — links Mc-Cullough to notions expressed on this campus forty-six years ago. In fact, he would have been a nice addition to the original group.

McCullough suggests that when we write, we find out what we do not know, implying that we should write to find out things. Addressing a different matter, he urges us to read letters, particularly those written by Flannery O'Connor. This is ironic because I have read some of O'Connor's letters, including one expressly relevant to the idea of writing as discovery. She wrote: "I don't know so well what I think until I see what I say" (1988, 5). This is an important concept, especially for students. Often, when a deadline is drawing near for, say, a term paper, students tell me that they have all of their ideas worked out inside their heads and just need to commit them to screen or paper. As you can probably guess, it almost never works out that way. They start, stop, double-check references, consult new material, restart, and revise. Perhaps some student has produced automatic writing in the mold of Yeats, but I see many more late papers than I see evidence of psychography. I certainly know how knowledge can be fashioned orally through speeches and dialogue, but the most complex representation of ideas will involve the kinds of revelations indicated by O'Connor.

The persistence of the belief that "I have it straight in my head" results, I surmise, from a Platonic view of the soul or the fact that we can subvocalize our intentions and become cognizant of that fact. That is why McCullough's exhortation to "rewrite, rewrite, and rewrite" is a welcome chant. It demystifies the writing process and affixes it not to the notion of gift but to the idea of regular and extended practice. If I don't have a forty-three-inch vertical leap or absolute pitch by the time I get to college, I am not going to gain those abilities while I am there. Many students feel this way about writing competently. If they think it is a gift and sense that they lack it, and we perpetuate the myth, then what is their motivation? I concede that brilliance may be an unusual talent, but competence is not. McCullough believes this firmly. Students could benefit from scavenging through the writer's drafts in the wastepaper basket or examining the rejected pages he pulls from his typewriter. It would be even better if he could explain to students the reasons that he discarded those pages. Students could also take advantage of any other drafts, including our own, that we share with them — anything that makes a manageable endeavor seem, in fact, manageable.

Beyond being committed to the idea that one learns to write by writing, McCullough offers additional advice that is noteworthy. For instance, he stresses the need for writers to read extensively. Surely, reading funds writing. I tell students that if they don't bank certain language funds, then they won't be there to withdraw. To be clear, I don't mean anything like a centralized bank. I certainly don't want to be attached to the "banking model" that Paulo Freire talked about as a way of illumining the authoritarian nature of classrooms in which teachers attempt to control the knowledge that is to be, in their view, parceled out to their charges (1970, 58). I'm thinking more of piggy banks, individual storehouses of linguistic resources — styles, perspectives, sense of rhythm, analysis frameworks, models that demonstrate how to solve problems encountered while writing. One can be in the middle of developing a narrative and trying to figure out how to move a character from a room on the fourth floor of an apartment building to a shop around the corner. Do you include all of the details that you could include — the number of stair steps, exact length of the lobby, number of paces to the corner, length of the strides, direction of the wind, velocity of the wind, and noise on the street? This harks back to the organizing function of writing. A quick glance at a published narrative may reveal that an accomplished writer resolved the issue with the simple line, "She rounded the corner five minutes later."

McCullough advises us to read our composed texts aloud as a way of obtaining a better feel for how the language is or is not working. This seems right to me, partly because I do it habitually. I cannot articulate the benefits in scientific terms, but it appears that reading aloud focuses attention in a different way than silent reading does and sometimes reveals discrepancies between intent and actual written production. Thus, reading aloud serves as a vital editing function.

A point on which we diverge a bit is the recommendation that aspiring and practicing writers read good writing. I won't try to adjudicate good or bad; we all have our tastes, and those tastes are culturally coded. But let's say that for the sake of argument we could agree on what constitutes good writing. In that case, I would assert that students and other writers should read as much of it as they can. I would also assert, though — and this is where I differ from McCullough — that they should periodically seek out bad writing, or what we might agree to call bad writing, as well. The novelist, poet, and journalist Richard Elman told me in a workshop many years ago that we could learn much from bad novels — namely, how to avoid writing them. His point has stuck with me and is connected in my mind with the idea that I expressed above about demystifying writing.

I suspect that we'll uncover other differences in our views about writing and writing instruction if we both talk long enough. I imagine McCullough to be more of a language prescriptivist than I am. However, I certainly applaud the manner in which he has pursued a writing career, and I appreciate that, recommendations notwithstanding, he articulates forcefully that there is more than one way to tackle what he calls "the good, hard work of writing well."

I'll conclude by sharing some of the fruits of McCullough's labor, items to which he directed me beforehand. The first is an early passage in his 1968 book, *The Johnstown Flood*:

> Again that morning there had been a bright frost in the hollow below the dam, and the sun was not up long before storm clouds rolled in from the southeast.
>
> By late afternoon a sharp, gusty wind was blowing down from the mountains, flattening the long grass along the lakeshore and kicking up tiny whitecaps out in the center of the lake. The big oaks and giant hemlocks, the hickories and black birch and sugar maples that crowded the hillside behind the summer colony began tossing back and forth, creaking and groaning. Broken branches and young leaves whipped through the air, and at the immense frame clubhouse that stood at the water's edge, halfway among the cottages, blue wood smoke trailed from great brick chimneys and vanished in fast swirls, almost as though the whole building, like a splendid yellow ark, were under steam, heading into the wind. (1968, 19)

Striking is the descriptive power, particularly the verbs: *rolled, flattening, kicking up, crowded, tossing, creaking, groaning, whipped, trailed, vanished, heading.* I always tell students that the use of vivid verbs compels attention. I surmise that at the remove of four decades McCullough wouldn't mind another go at "had been," "was," and "was blowing," fairly bland usage that fails to match the passage's overall standard. He advocates letting material sit so that we can return to it with a slightly different view, though I don't think he was referring to forty-four-year time spans.

A second selection, drawn from his 2011 book, *The Greater Journey*, illustrates the importance of selecting details as an aid to precision. Regarding an incident involving Charles Moulton, Mc-

Cullough writes: "Small, slight, and bespectacled, he was hardly an imposing figure, and, against the backdrop of the enormous house, he seemed smaller still" (316). Through the brief but effectively detailed comparison, we can visualize Moulton. I have not asked McCullough why he suggested these samples, among a few others. But overall they seem to me admirable outcomes of a writer at work. More to the point, McCullough's career is an excellent example of the successful writer's pursuit — the steady and steadfast progression of claiming insights by mastering a particular verbal code, the exploration as well as shaping of contexts, the satisfaction of self-revelation through prose, and the restless search for greater clarity. And if acclaim is headed a writer's way, he or she, as Barthes and Summerfield knew, will not likely attempt to dodge it.

REFERENCES

Barthes, Roland. 1972. "Literature and Signification." In Roland Barthes, *Critical Essays* translated by Richard Howard, 261–79. Evanston, IL: Northwestern University Press.

Britton, James. 1982. "Writing to Learn and Learning to Write." In *Prospect and Retrospect: Selected Essays of James Britton*, edited by Gordon M. Pradl, 94–111. Montclair, NJ: Boynton/Cook.

Dixon, John. 1967. *Growth through English*. London: National Association for the Teaching of English.

Freire, Paulo. 1970. *Pedagogy of the Oppressed*. Translated by Myra Bergman Ramos. New York: Continuum.

McCullough, David. 1968. *The Johnstown Flood*. New York: Simon and Schuster.

———. 2011. *The Greater Journey: Americans in Paris*. New York: Simon and Schuster.

O'Connor, Flannery. 1988. "Letter to Elizabeth McKee on June 19, 1948." In Flannery O'Connor, *The Habit of Being: Letters*, edited by Sally Fitzgerald, 4–5. Paperback ed. New York: Farrar, Straus, & Giroux.

LESLIE BUTLER

six History as a Laboratory for the Good, Hard Work of Writing Well

There is much to agree with and admire in David McCullough's comments on writing, especially his exhortation to aspiring writers to read good writing. With that in mind, let me start by saying what a joy it has been for me to spend time reading McCullough's own writing. I can only hope that I have thereby absorbed some small measure of his talent and artistry.

History has a particular relationship to writing, stemming perhaps from its own history as a body of knowledge. Although Dartmouth considers history a social science, at many other institutions history joins the ranks of the humanities. And in actuality, history as a discipline has a somewhat awkward relationship to the other social sciences, which seem less frequently to employ words like "craft" or "art" to describe their practice. History is what we might call a predisciplinary discipline. Unlike the other social sciences — political science, anthropology, psychology, and sociology — which were "invented" in the nineteenth century, history precedes by centuries the whole concept of disciplines, let alone the modern university. The craft of history began when humanity began, as a storytelling function by which communities remembered the past, nurtured collective identities, and inspired noble futures. It is, then, no accident that in many Germanic and Romance languages, the words for history and story are the same (for example, the French *histoire* or the German *Geschichte*).

History as a discipline in the modern research university has of course traveled far from its storytelling origins, but in many ways it still bears traces of those origins. Consider, for example, how much McCullough's comments on writing sound like advice for aspiring novelists as well as historians. "Beginnings are crucial," he tells us. Don't forget that "your subjects were real human beings" and "show their strengths, their failings." "Remember the five senses," he urges. Show, don't tell. His books, which are often said to read like novels and one of which was turned into an award-winning HBO miniseries, amply show (not tell) what he means by this.

Anyone who has read McCullough's work knows that the man can set a scene. His most recent book, *The Greater Journey*, gives the reader a palpable sense of how dangerous and difficult transatlantic travel could be in the 1830s. We watch as poor Charles Sumner, the future antislavery senator of Massachusetts, spends nearly four days prostrate in his cabin, unable to eat or read, let alone walk about. But for those who made it safely to Paris, the rewards were plenty, as McCullough shows when he vividly recreates a first encounter with breakfast in a Parisian hotel. Here he is quoting the writer Nathaniel Willis ("let your characters speak for themselves as often as possible"): "There are few things bought with money that are more delightful than a French breakfast. . . . [I]t appears in the shape of two small vessels, one of coffee and one of hot milk, two kinds of bread, with a thin, printed slice of butter. . . . The coffee has an aroma peculiarly exquisite, something quite different than any I have ever tasted before" (2011, 27). All five of one's senses are engaged, and one's mouth practically starts watering while imagining that first café au lait.

McCullough develops even his secondary characters in fully human and memorable detail. Surely no one who has read *The Path between the Seas* can forget the brilliant and cunning Vicomte Ferdinand de Lesseps, the Frenchman who built the Suez Canal but whose dreams of glory were transformed into a decade-long nightmare in Panama. Everything de Lesseps — as well as his son and hundreds of other French investors — invested in the project disappeared in the face of the mountainous terrain, recurrent landslides, and deadly waves of malaria and yellow fever he encountered.

Even when they do not write as beautifully as McCullough, historians at times resemble novelists. They grapple with the complexity of human motivation and the irony of unintended consequences. They work to see events from multiple perspectives, striving to enter empathetically into the worlds of others — even those with whom they disagree — at least enough to understand them. Historians cultivate an eye for the telling detail and an ear for the evocative quotation. They inescapably think about narrative when writing, if only because they must consider how much the choice of where to begin and end a story does to shape its meaning.

But of course historians are not novelists. They are constrained by facts and by the limits of evidence. In recent decades, some historians have pushed at the outer edges of those limits, turning history into a laboratory for writing and the narrative form into a meditation on historical knowledge. Richard Wightman Fox's *Trials of Intimacy* (1999) ponders the reliability of sources by following the extensive paper trail of a notorious adultery trial in reverse chronological order. In *The Unredeemed Captive* (1994), about the aftermath of a 1704 Indian raid on Deerfield, Massachusetts, John Demos tests the limits of the knowable, venturing into carefully earned (and scrupulously demarcated) speculation about human motivations and emotions. Linda Gordon alternates between gripping narrative chapters and analytical and contextual chapters to tell the story of *The Great Arizona*

Orphan Abduction (1999). These three notable examples, all by established and well-respected scholars, are not typical of professional history writing, but they do reveal some of the discipline's creative approach to writing.

Still, most professional historians do not write in either experimentally postmodern or even conventionally narrative ways. So I want to conclude by drawing a distinction, which I think is easily and often elided in discussions of historical writing, between narrative writing and good writing. These are not synonymous terms. I can think of countless examples of excellent writing, especially in my own field of American history: writing that is less rooted in storytelling than in analysis and argument, but that is not necessarily less "good" because of this.

The kind of writing I have in mind may not read like a novel, but it can be powerfully readable nonetheless. Consider the introductions to these three different books, written in different decades but all important works in the field. Edmund Morgan wrote in his classic *American Slavery, American Freedom*: "[This book] is the story of how one set of Americans arrived at the American paradox, an attempt to see how slavery and freedom made their way to England's first American colony and grew there together, the one supporting the other" (1975, 6). Daniel Rodgers wrote in *Contested Truths*: "This is a book about political words — an inquiry into the language of argument in the American past through a handful of the keywords which have boomed and rattled through American politics since independence." (1987, 3). And Jill Lepore wrote in *The Name of War*: "This is a study of war, and of how people write about it. Writing about war can be almost as difficult as waging it and, often enough, is essential to winning it" (1998, ix). No stories here, yet all three introductions effectively engage the reader on both aesthetic and intellectual levels. That is, the writing sounds good to the ear, but it also provokes the reader to think about the subject matter to follow.

This analytical and argumentative writing is the kind of writing our students are often asked to do. We ask them to synthesize large amounts of data, to explain long-term processes, to interpret different kinds of sources, to assess the often conflicting interpretations of other scholars, to frame historical problems in theoretical terms, to distinguish between cause and effect, to construct arguments and marshal evidence to support those arguments, and to demonstrate how they arrived at their conclusions. Many of these analytical tasks do not lend themselves to a narrative style of writing. Colorful characters may not play a role at all; the five senses may not be enlisted. Sometimes a reader must be told as well as shown — shown with compelling evidence, certainly, but told in clear, forceful prose.

But, again, much of what McCullough has to say about "the good, hard work of writing well" applies in these cases nonetheless. Perhaps even more than elsewhere. Convincing arguments usually require skillful writing, and superb analysis can only be aided by clear prose. Working hard at writing well is as important for the writer as it is for the reader, for — as McCullough aptly observes — "writing focuses the brain like nothing else." Although clear writing does not always reflect clear thinking, muddled writing usually does betray muddled thinking.

Some of our students work hard at writing important and engaging stories about history. But I want all of our students (and faculty members) to hold all their writing to a high standard of clarity and vigor and not to use the fact that they are not writing narrative as an excuse not to have to think about writing. I would like them to internalize principles of good historical writing (from using strong verbs in the active voice to fitting their arguments to the evidence) and learn the importance of editing their own work and constantly revising it. I would like them to become self-conscious about their writing and to take into account the needs of their readers. I would like them to recognize that the more they come to care about writing, the more difficult it will actually become — precisely because they care. In short, I would like them to agree with McCullough that writing well is good and hard work.

REFERENCES

Demos, John. 1994. *The Unredeemed Captive: A Family Story from Early America* New York: Knopf.

Fox, Richard Wightman. 1999. *Trials of Intimacy: Loss and Love in the Beecher-Tilton Scandal.*Chicago: University of Chicago Press.

Gordon, Linda. 1999. *The Great Arizona Orphan Abduction.* Cambridge, MA: Harvard University Press.

Lepore, Jill. 1998. *The Name of War: King Philip's War and the Origins of American Identity* New York: Knopf.

McCullough, David. 2011. *The Greater Journey: Americans in Paris.* New York: Simon and Schuster.

Morgan, Edmund S. 1975. *American Slavery, American Freedom: The Ordeal of Colonial Virginia*New York: W. W. Norton.

Rodgers, Daniel T. 1987. *Contested Truths: Keywords in American Politics since Independence.* Cambridge, MA: Harvard University Press.

part 3 Interdisciplinary Studies

seven Writing and States of Emergency

After my initial rush of enthusiasm about participating in this project had subsided, I realized, almost in a kind of terror, that having to address my writing process out loud or in print was, for me, tantamount to having to respond in public to queries about my sex life. This stunning revelation explains why, all of a sudden, words took flight out the nearest window. But with the ensuing crisis of silence came an essential clue: that is, the extent to which writing for me is the basis of my living. I would even go so far as to say that writing has defined for more than three decades now the very stakes of my living — both the bread and the hunger of it. To analogize the writing process to states of emergency, then, opens the way for me to think systematically about the relationship between the social, political, and historical context of my professional career and that perpendicular pronoun, "I." Furthermore, the analogy highlights the central paradox of writing and study in the humanities: wherever "I" is located with regard to its object brings subjective and objective dimensions into convergence. In fact, the distinction may well collapse when the critic, for instance, strains to see the difference between how she demarks her object and the object itself. To say that the difference goes away brings into sharper focus the autobiographical import of writing, which gives the latter its edge, its human interest. In other words, topics of investigation find their meaning to the extent that an individual signature infuses them; to the degree that an inertia, some stubborn hardness in the quality of things or events, has been penetrated at last by the heat of curiosity, or the sheer magic of effort.

The initial observation that I would make about writing — an actual physical act that could be described as tension that is bodily felt and not finished or relieved until the tension is resolved — is the last step that I will address concerning a process that the writer is never sure will succeed. But we have now to do with beginnings: writing for me always begins in, belongs to a perceived historical juncture, insofar as it is neither timeless nor neutral. It has already been defined in part by forces beyond the writer's control and manipulation, even if it seems that such is not the case. As a result, the writer is implicated in an outcome, however hidden or recessed a narrativizing voice may appear to be. The writer's awareness of context — which encompasses not only a putative audience but also the conditions that allow certain questions to be asked, certain assumptions to be understood as more or less stable — differs across a range of pressures, from disciplinary postures to what the writer perceives as her own location. Consequently, the writer is never advancing in isolation but, rather, in the sociality of belonging to a world shaped by a synthesis of forces that precede particular gestures of response. There are few topics that we can address today in the humanities that do not take into account how the subject of writing has been transformed by radical shifts of gravity in what counts as knowledge in the contemporary period. One cannot write, for instance, as though what Robyn Wiegman calls "identity knowledge"[1] (2012, 1) has not destabilized both our objects and how we see them, as well as how the one who would write must position herself in relationship to those shifting currents of enunciation and opinion.

My writing career began in the early 1970s, a period that includes the immediate aftermath of the civil rights movement in the United States, as well as the post-Vietnam years. As graduate students at the time, my generation of doctoral candidates had just lived through one of the most sustained periods of political activism in the nation's history, a period of cultural synthesis that had called for the opening of the public university, North and South, to the children of citizens and taxpayers across the color line. Practically speaking, the young, like myself, were positioned on a kind of frontier, and what is normally regarded as a peaceful proceeding — attending classes and establishing contact with professors and other students — was suddenly fraught with uncertainty. In some cases, especially in the South, the proceeding was accompanied by the threat of injury, bodily and otherwise. Leaving the South and travelling to Massachusetts for doctoral study, I arrived on a scene no less fraught, albeit for different reasons, but nonetheless more broadly involved in political expression: demonstrations against the American military involvement in Vietnam, for instance, ran along lines exactly parallel to black students' agitation on the campus of Brandeis University where I was enrolled. Although the immediate threat to life and limb, which had characterized my years as an undergraduate at the University of Memphis, had significantly subsided, I still felt compelled to choose to be engaged by the issues of the day. Consequently, I came to writing as an *autobiographical* subject, displaced onto academic ground. "Displacement" is a key term here because I had to find a way to insert and assert this "I" in the languages available to the academy. What I was writing and choosing to write was not *autobiographical* per se, but the writing found its moment and urgency in my response to the political movement bearing down on the university. I would, then, describe my positioning or location as a subject along a dual (and dueling?) axis: the politics of movement from a putative outside and an institutional politics from a putative inside. This placed me between contending claims that would be difficult to reconcile, divided as they were across the fault lines of race.

The imperative to translate from one axis to the other defined the task of writing as I encountered it, to translate the politics of movement into a curricular object, and then to articulate the new object as political and creative practice in the world. This task, as lonely as it felt, was not mine singly; rather, it characterized the project of an entire generation of black intellectuals born within earshot of totalitarian regimes abroad and the terrors of racial apartheid at home. From this angle, especially with regard to racial and cultural questions, which have been most urgent for me, writing is either a discomfiting choice, or one does not engage it at all. To call such choosing uncomfortable, to say that it is accompanied by its own particular anxieties, is not to argue that writing under such conditions is without pleasure, even humor at times, but it is to contend that writing is marked in one's own mind as a form of risk taking that requires the subject of it to take cover from time to time. This going up against — in my case, some of the discourses that constitute knowledge in the academy and the assumptions that hold them in place — essentially describes my orientation as a scholar and writer. But in another sense, the discourses already in place enabled my scholarly work: my antagonistic stance toward them could never be absolute and, in fact, could not have existed without these points of anchor. Instead, my stance was contrarian or contrastive in my desire to make use of them — literary criticism and theory, primarily — as a way to bring out what I perceived as some of the missing elements of interlocution. The relationship that came about as a result might be thought of as an instance of *cooperative antagonism* between the stable features of a disciplinary protocol and *emergent scholarly interests*.

When I set out to produce a dissertation in the early to mid-

1970s on the rhetoric of black sermons in the Protestant tradition, there were not many obvious places to search for secondary scholarship on the subject. In other words, the black sermon in its rhetorical configurations identified an emergent field of scholarship, primarily inspired by the powerful use of the sermonic form in the hands of the Reverend Martin Luther King, Jr., and his colleagues of the Southern Christian Leadership Conference. After all, black sermonic form, displaced onto decidedly political ground, had helped to produce changes we could only have dreamed in the aftermath of World War II and the anticommunist initiatives of the so-called scoundrel time. If the power of speech was so transformative, hadn't one better have a look at a particular iteration? Beyond the archives of the sermons themselves, both the living archive and the archive of the special collection, scholarship on the matter was, for all intents and purposes, inchoate, even though sociological and historical studies of black religious expression were available by way of W. E. B. Du Bois's and E. Franklin Frazier's well-known work, among others. But my own mandate to update the critical and theoretical picture could have started only from these impression points, which carried me just so far. As the daughter of deacons of the southern black Baptist church, I had stored an infinite number of sermon performances in my memory, but memory in this case was a far cry from the scholar's bibliography, or a body of material on which to work. I learned only later, in the course of further research on the sermon beyond the stage of the dissertation, that there were mother lodes of black sermons, stretching back to the genre of meditation in the seventeenth century, stored in the special collections of at least two substantial archival holdings on the East Coast alone. And of course the black sermon is still produced all the time in urban and rural settings across the country. In an institutional framework for which "the sermon" meant John

Donne's exquisite seventeenth-century addresses delivered at St. Paul's Cathedral in London or the admonitory articulations of Cotton Mather and Jonathan Edwards in colonial America, the rhetoric of black sermons of any time and place were exotic fare indeed. I would be justified in saying, then, that I had to tinker my way to both the object to work on and the methods of procedure by which to bring it to stand.

The enterprise of bricolage – essentially, making use of whatever one finds at hand – became my own in this work that essayed to explain black preaching. The sample at the time, now associated with music, had no formal name or recognition, but the dissertation's table of contents reveals it as a strategy of procedure – an example of a sermon from nineteenth-century Virginia, an analysis of James Baldwin's prose in *Go Tell It on the Mountain*, a reading of the recorded sermons on the old Chess label of the Reverend C. L. Franklin, and two instances of contemporary preaching performance that included a foray into the significance of the urban landscape to sermonic reception all intermingled their thematic chords across the surface of "Fabrics of History: Essays on the Black Sermon." What I did not know at the time was that this *mezclada* or mixture of elements presented a problem of genre. However, the latter, in time, would be absorbed by my professional field in the guise of interdisciplinarity a decade or so later. The results were not only unwelcome to editors at publishing houses (about twelve rejection letters are buried somewhere in my personal archives), but also to English departments in the general way that black studies would be subject to a hostile reception for the first decade and a half of its academic career on predominantly white campuses across the United States. I recall now with a modicum of amusement that one colleague, a historian herself, expressed surprise that black preaching had a history to be gathered, or a theory to be projected, in the first place!

Even though the work itself aims to describe sermonic phenomena with as much precision as possible, "Fabrics of History" wanted to do more: in the writing, I was interested in talking to neighboring fields of discourse in literary criticism and narrative theory. The precarious bridge between my topic and its neighbors was provided by Vladimir Propp's study of fairy tales (translated from the Russian in 1968) in isolating repetitive elements in the sermon. "The Eagle Stirs Her Nest," for instance, a sermon that appears in the repertoire of many generations of preachers, acts like an oral tale insofar as it shows traces and patterns of inherited formulae of locution, as well as signature moves that belong to particular speakers. This aspect of legacy identifies the black sermon as an extranarrative production that relies on the improvisational move to drive it across the chasms of time and space. As a result, it participates in anonymity as well as the egoistic drive of mortal speakers. As prose performance, the sermon crosses its wires with poetry, to the extent that today's performer resembles those of his father's generation in making his way up and down the plot line of the sermon with some of the same sort of rhetorical and narrative tools. What I aimed at in "Fabrics of History" was the expression of my own belief in the lyrical, conceptual, and narrative power of preaching, which came to define a human community in its moments of crisis and beyond. On the one hand, there was black studies, relatively new to the academic world and an object of constant doubt and suspicion; on the other hand, there were literary criticism and theory, which inscribed one of the most prestigious tracks of humanistic study in the modern academy and one that was only occasionally open to doubt. Poised between this Scylla and Charybdis of enunciative possibility, my generation set out to make work that would qualify as a kind of port of call in a contact zone of critical inquiry. What seemed to be required was that one hit the ground running or — sticking with the metaphor — learn to write under conditions of emergency, when writing remains the measure of the human under the old Enlightenment rules.

What that looks like *as writing* is hard to say, but perhaps we might begin with the motive of *irritation*. Already given the status of minority (and for reasons that have to do with more than, and other than, numbers), the academy's new demographic group, now inhabiting an unwonted and uncustomary space inside, was summoned to prove its worthiness to stake a legitimate intellectual claim. This provocation sums up the new relationship — it is basically the beginning of wisdom in such a maelstrom — as an emergency, given that the totality of the institution's public and private functions now had to accommodate difference (presumed and actual) in its calculations of a putative sameness. This was not easy going for either the new minority demographic cohorts or the traditional ones of the institution, and it is fair to say that *being irritated* was a universally shared condition. But members of the minority might well have had an advantage in the circumstances, precisely because they had everything to prove. In writing, then, one could aspire to a kind of posture of the gadfly — a systematic "worrying the line,"[2] as Cheryl Wall (2005) defines it, by relocating the center of gravity with the introduction of new topics to the scholarly dialogue, testing canons of value and the assumptions that hold them in place, and, above all, working at the level of the sentence to dislodge clichés and install idiomatic address in their place. As I see it, my collection of essays, *Black, White, and in Color*, (2003), devotes its energies to the first and third elements of this repertory of ambitions.

To take a couple of the essays as a test case, I would say that neither the introduction to the volume, "Peter's Pans: Eating in the Diaspora," nor "Moving on Down the Line: Variations on the African-American Sermon," a follow-up essay to my dissertation, belongs to any one school of criticism and theory but, rather, borrows its ways and means from a few of them that would meet the requirements of intersectional work. To that extent, the essays, as well as the volume itself, might be said to be experimental.

"Moving on Down the Line," which investigates representative instances of the sermon archive before recorded sound (around 1918), opens with a contrastive move that juxtaposes disparate styles of worship or pursues the opposition between hierarchical and demotic modes of religious address. In short, I wanted to evoke, in the former instance, the implicit history of those forms of worship that accompany the elaborate ritualistic content of high-church formation and in the latter, those that characterize Protestant modes of address. The differences between these forms are not by any means absolute, of course, but they are solid enough to make it possible to drive a decisive contrast between the forms. My comparison was suggested by Henry Adams's meditations on the architecture of two European venues — Mont St. Michel and Chartres — in his seminal study of these two famous cathedrals (1959).[3] Compared to Protestant churches, the European cathedrals provide a feast for the eye in their sweeping enormous mass of brick and stone. In contrast, the abiding centrality of the sermon, performed against simpler patterns and materials of construction in the Protestant sample, captures the ear, an approach that seems to be precisely coordinated with the dismantling of hierarchy in the interest of placing the individual soul in direct and unmediated contact with notions of the divine. My sustained engagement with the figures of difference in this case was driven by what I know about the architecture of small Protestant churches and my occasional visits to cathedrals in European and American cities. The point of the essay was not only to express my astonishment at the dramatic relationship between material construction and spiritual purpose, but also to sketch out the sensual dimensions of the individual's place in this calculus of motives. In other words, for all the publicness of places of worship, there is always a subjective response to their size, look, and relationship to human scale. Working through contrasts between ear and eye, familiar and unfamiliar landscapes, and the implied disparity of economic means among church organizations, I wanted the emphasis to fall on the black church and the import of the word. The latter warranted dramatic highlighting because the word was denied in the historic instance of the cultural apprenticeship of African Americans. In this case, literacy, perhaps for the first time in modern history, became a matter of life and death. Literacy was not simply a nice thing to achieve, but it often made the decisive difference between subjugation and self-sovereignty. The word play that is embedded in the title of the essay — adopted from a popular tune of the 1960s, as well as referring to the act of reading itself — is meant to suggest that between the lines of scripture, "the narratives of insurgence are delivered" (Spillers 2003, 252). In the nature of the case, religious expression, displaced onto the immediate ground of the here and now, describes an emergency with all bets off — one could well lose one's life. The sermon, in its sensitivity to what is at stake, is designed to transport the hearer to the other side of disaster — in short, into the future of possibility. It was this narrative, in its layered historical vocation, that the essay attempted to trace by way of autobiographical references; figures of paronomasia; and the unwonted, if not unwarranted, confrontation of cultural contrarieties — in other words, a chance afternoon visit one summer day to Milan's Il Duomo de San Carlo had provoked my recall of something else, both dissonant and related.

If pursued with sufficient discipline, writing acquires its own powers of instruction — in other words, one act leads to another with foreshortened tendencies in the writer to be terrorized by the open (or blank) page; but learning to keep going is the price that the discipline of writing exacts. One has to trust a hunch or inspiration in the sheer coldness of writerly solitude (The gnomes of professional competence whisper, "It can't be done, it shouldn't be done!" So much for courage). But I would regard my entire career as a writer – and I suspect that I am not alone in this – as a struggle against a procedural rightness or what is expected of the scholarly disposition. "Moving on Down the Line" and other essays written between the mid-1970s and early twentieth century might be described, collectively, as a token of just such a struggle. The hope is to forge an individual response to a critical problematic, to remain true to the broad outlines of an object separate from oneself that comes into view, and to re-configure an apparent conceptual impasse as the genesis of new movement – that is, the enslavement of women as a situation for feminist, as well as race-bound, inquiry (I am thinking here of "Mama's Baby, Papa's Maybe: An American Grammar Book" and "'The Permanent Obliquity of an In(pha)llibly Straight': In the Time of the Daughters and the Fathers," among others). All of these essays attempt to break through a perceptual cramp that complements and accompanies the entire archive, both imagistic and scriptive, of cross- and intra-racial discourses (at least as I read the matter) as we have inherited it from the past, especially as the latter pertains to black culture and subjectivity. Such an effort is not without a stab at humor.

The introduction to *Black, White, and in Color*, "Peter's Pans," combines the title of a lecture that I once delivered and a tribute to a dear friend (with the sobriquet "Peter") who was a Florida restaurateur for a number of years; there is also the obvious riff on J. M. Barrie's *Peter Pan*, the tale of the magical boy who swallowed a complicated clock. The pluralization in the title doubles the function of the essay as an allusion to H. D. "Peter" Briggs's savory morsels, as well as to the variety of the palate offered to the traveller making her way across the African diaspora. In its figurative disposition as an instance of rhetorical "double supply," "Peter's Pans" brings food into view as a plausible element of cultural analysis as it gestures toward the mix of cultures and ethnicities that traverse the geopolitical sum of dispersed African-descended populations in the modern era. "Peter's Pans" takes into account the food ways experienced by a single traveller in selected cities of the United States, Canada, the Caribbean, Europe, and West Africa, a distinct itinerary that first materialized in the modern world by way of the historic Middle Passage of the Atlantic slave trade, which began in the fifteenth century. But to interrupt the solemnity of this tragic theme, at least in this particular instance of writing, I wanted to point to the jollity and pleasure of eating, starting with the mock-serious line that begins the essay: "When I think on the stunning alimentation of an egg, I come face to face with one of the miracles of human existence" (Spillers 2003, 1). The egg is one of my favorite foods, and — in its inimitable elegance and simplicity as a statement of excellent organic design — stirs up imaginative commotions when one considers what it can be translated into: meringues; the solid food of the Easter egg hunt and the devilled egg of delicious hors d'oeuvres; a liquid state, mixed with juices; and the disappearing atoms in a chef's patent-leather black chocolate cake or turkey dressing made with sage. But the tricky egg also sustains another dimension of meaning as the origin of a variety of species, as well as a handy figurative implement available to writers (as Faulkner well knew) as a miniature elliptical orb that mimics the shape of the cartographer's and astronomer's globe. If we could transport the egg to the mythical Mt. Olympus, then it might well turn up among the principal viatica of Mercury, the fabulous shape shifter. Lastly, the "pans" in the title offer another way to identify the potpourri of essays that makes up the collection in the word's reference to the black problematic in its material and cultural situatedness. The essay's blend of seriousness and play brought me closer to the dialogic interweaving that writing might, on any given day, strive to accomplish.

"'All the Things You Could Be by Now If Sigmund Freud's Wife Was Your Mother': Psychoanalysis and Race" attempts to create a similar porosity of motives that shuttle their way among contrastive aims. The essay questions to what extent psychoanalytic protocols might be deployed in contexts that diverge from those protocols' cultural and historical provenance. Deciding that this inquiry could not helpfully result in a simple yes or no, I followed a rather circuitous path through a few well-known examples of research in the psychoanalytic field, starting with the work of Freud, Jacques Lacan, and Frantz Fanon and proceeding through currents of African anthropological thought. The essay ends on a note of conjecture, which might possibly introduce an innovative idea to the discussion: If the plot of an Oedipal struggle between African generations was interrupted by the Atlantic slave trade, what are the cultural implications of such an outcome on either side of the Atlantic? If the delay is constantly reinforced by elements that deflect the attention away from the historic break, we might have to settle for a suspended resolution (where we appear to reside today) that bears the name of "race" — or, more precisely, the *racialized subjectivity* of African subjects in the New World. In this case, the would-be search for the father is displaced onto an instance of emergency that puts the emphasis elsewhere or throws the subject onto an altogether new path of humanation. The twists and turns that the essay necessarily performs seemed to me best analogized to a complicated piece of music from the jazz repertoire — the bassist Charles Mingus's "All the Things You Could Be by Now If Sigmund Freud's Wife Was Your Mother," which lends the essay its title. I also wanted to signal that the answers that I was seeking could be supplied only by practitioners of psychoanalysis. As a lay person with an interest in psychoanalytic theory, I went about the business of the essay with the disciplinary tools most readily available to me — that is, a commitment to reading engendered by the practices of literary criticism and theory. In other words, I wanted to make clear the psychoanalytic problematic for black culture from the point of view of a single layman, coming to the matter from a nonspecialist site.

Readers will be able to gauge the outcome for themselves. But for me, the writing of the essay (as well as others in the volume) yielded a modicum of satisfaction because the tension that I felt in approaching the work was relieved. This conclusion is not to say that the essays could not be improved by more time and knowledge, but, rather, that the period inscribed by this particular attempt at writing *felt* finished. To my mind, this sense of an ending begins to answer the question put by my Dartmouth interlocutors — "How do you know when you are writing well?" Quite simply, the writer never really knows (nor ever will) if she is, in fact, writing well. If she did, the good offices of editors and of readers not at all invested in the writing would have no point. What I can say, though, is that the writing, from the writer's point of view, must respond to the pulse of the nerves — must answer the summons of the body — that strains toward the quieting of impulses set in motion by curiosity, suspicion, or the unrest of dissatisfaction. The worrisome delay in finishing this piece of writing, for example, offers a prime case in point: the number of repented and withdrawn pages would nearly equal those in a legal pad precisely because they did not meet the test of satisfaction, or what the passages sounded like in the ear and to the mind the next day, and the nagging sensation that something was said too ponderously or boringly, or edged toward the dishonest, or even ended up too coy and cute by half! I would submit — and will acknowledge that I do not know quite how this happens — that the body mysteriously aids the writing writer by telling her that the path of anguish has reached its destination for now. For this reason, I would say, furthermore, that the writer's relationship to her body changes in the shift from the surface of a blank piece of paper to that of a blank computer screen, although I would need far more technological expertise to even guess how or why this seems to be the case. Perhaps this experience sustains only generational bearing and nothing more, but my hunch runs counter to this conclusion. On paper, it seems to me that one confronts only the silence of one's thoughts and their failure or success at keeping going. In contrast, with the screen, the blinking cursor and other signals winking at the margins of the frame behave rather like a bad traffic cop who urges motorists to hurry up, despite the conditions of the road. These subliminal charges and vectors that disrupt the body's own puzzles and haltings seem to overwhelm the processes of writing by deflecting attention to the *technology* of production and away from the production itself. In some ways, the scratch of the pen, under my control, is comforting, insofar as it is the only thing that tells me I'm still here, even when it stops. In any case, writing as we know it today appears to be organically related to the electricity that flows between one's inner commotions and the closest or most intimate outside surface. For me, this means the words as they pour out directly in front of me rather than as translated to my eyesight by way of an interface. Perhaps I also make it clear here only exactly how old I am!

In any case, I would regard my career as an academic writer as the effort to balance the impulsive claims of writing against the demands of a scholarly regimen. Perhaps the desire to write fiction, which I relinquished at one time in the interest of earning tenure but which remains a hoped-for space of return at some future time, has seeped into my academic ambitions to produce neither fish nor fowl, even though one colleague has suggested to me that my criticism is fiction! Not knowing whether to be embarrassed or flattered by this suggestion, I should hope that I have gained some insight into my creative ways and means by way of the cryptic message of one of my graduate school professors, J. V. Cunningham, who spoke one day in his American poetry seminar about the abiding centrality of the word and its relationship to idiomatic expression. I've never forgotten the remark, although it would have been typical of me at the time *not* to have asked him what he meant, intimidated as I was by his cold, monosyllabic conciseness. However, I think that I have given the concept a meaning of my own, which is to work toward idiomatic address. The need to break through the surface of the already read, already known, and already presumed about articulates conditions that accompanied my birth because of the color of my skin, because of my sexual plumbing, as it were. These conditions are the supports that appear to have come trailing the natural order of things. From that point of view, to have discovered this imperative as a student and scholar some time ago was to confront the emergency and its states that intellectual life takes as its task. Writing here is to assume one of the guises of struggle and engagement — words, words, words.

NOTES

1. In her important text on critical and theoretical developments in the human sciences over the last three decades, Robyn Wiegman examines "identity knowledges" in reference "to many projects of academic study that were institutionalized in the U.S. university in the twentieth century for the study of identity" (2012, 1) — gender and women's studies; critical

race theory and African American literature; Chicano/a studies; lesbian, gay, bisexual, and transgender studies; Native American studies; and postcolonial studies chief among them.

2. Cheryl Wall adopts "worrying the line" for the title for her study of black women writers in the latter half of the twentieth century. A blues trope, the locution identifies changes in stress and pitch in a passage of blues that repeats a given line. As a metaphor for writing, the locution points to variations on a plethora of narrative themes and schemes (2005, 8).

3. Privately printed in 1904, Henry Adams's *Mont St. Michel and Chartres* was not published until 1913. In 1959, Doubleday Anchor Books released an edition with an introduction by Ralph Adams Cram.

REFERENCES

Adams, Henry. 1959. *Mont-Saint-Michel and Chartres*. With an introduction by Ralph Adams Cram. Garden City, NY: Doubleday Anchor.

Propp, Vladimir. 1968. *Morphology of the Folktale*. Translated by Laurence Scott. Austin: University of Texas Press.

Spillers, Hortense J. 2003. *Black, White, and in Color: Essays on American Literature and Culture*. Chicago: University of Chicago Press.

Wall, Cheryl A. 2005. *Worrying the Line: Black Women Writers, Lineage, and Literary Tradition*. Chapel Hill: University of North Carolina Press.

Wiegman, Robyn. 2012. *Object Lessons*. Durham, NC: Duke University Press.

PATRICIA BIZZELL

eight Her Prophetic Voice

A Response to Hortense Spillers

Max Weber's essay "Science as a Vocation" is a *locus classicus* of the traditional orientation to academic work imported into the United States from Germany in the late nineteenth century. According to Weber, the serious academic should be a disinterested inquirer, someone who only analyzes questions of value but never takes a stand on them. For an academic to indicate his own value preferences, says Weber, would be unmanly [*sic*] (1958). To go further and promulgate values from the lectern is to set oneself up as a false prophet — very bad. One may turn to religion in private, says Weber, to solace oneself for the moral aridity of one's scholarly life. But morality should have nothing to do with one's academic work.

By Weber's standards, Hortense Spillers does everything wrong! If ever there were a prophetic voice in the halls of academe, it is hers. She positions the genesis of her writing career in the context of important moral battles, over the Vietnam War and over the movement to win full civil rights for people of African descent. This, indeed, is writing in response to states of emergency. Spillers dedicates her academic work to bringing those on the "outside" of the traditional academy into the "inside," as for example in the groundbreaking collection of essays she edited with Marjorie Pryse, *Conjuring* (1985), in which she speaks frankly about the power of the academy to foster the creative work of black women writers by teaching their literature and, in many cases, by employing these writers as teachers, too. As she puts it in the final essay in that volume, here "the academy meets life, and life the academy," transforming the word "tradition" into an "active verb" (1985a, 260).

Certainly the conditions of social injustice in the United States constitute a state of "emergency," and if scholarly writing can do anything to alleviate this emergency, it is certainly "urgent" to do so. At the very least, scholarship can bring sustained attention to material previously deemed unworthy of it. If Spillers's scholarship can bring attention to black women's fiction, previously deemed unworthy because unsuited to New Critical literary analysis, perhaps the insights into African American life that this literature offers will inform and inspire many people to fight for the same social causes that motivate Spillers. All I can say is, I hope so!

Contra Weber, Spillers asserts — and now I'm quoting from the notes she sent Christiane Donahue before our conference — that "all writing is situated in an historical juncture; insofar as it is so, writing is neither timeless, nor neutral. As a result, the writer is *always* implicated in a writing outcome" (emphasis in original). Implicated, that is, politically, morally, and personally. Of course, in traditional academic writing (writing in which "tradition" is intransitive), the writer's implicit stake is concealed behind passive voice constructions. Spillers contests this concealment with the free use of what she calls the "perpendicular pronoun," the "I."

Few modern developments in academic discourse have had and will have effects as dramatic as the emergence of the first person. Simply by saying "I," the writer owns his or her scholarship in a brand-new way. Following the perpendicular pronoun, we find physical space, geographical space, and human embodiment entering into scholarly writing as well, even in method, as Spillers indicates in her remarks on preferring to write her drafts in longhand. We also find, for example, that Spillers opens her essay on a Paule Marshall novel (1985b) by describing how its Caribbean island setting looks when approached by sea — creating the impression that Spillers has been there. Weber would say, Why should that matter? Or, to give another example, we find the rhetorician Malea Powell (2002) describing her ritual tattoos by way of explaining how she integrates her American Indian perspective into her academic writing. Weber would probably say, how rude!

Spillers's work has been innovative in another way, too, which helps to explain why her presentation is located in the conference program under "interdisciplinary approaches." African American studies' and other scholarly ethnic studies' approaches have required that materials and methods from previously distinct academic disciplines, such as literary studies, history, psychology, and religious studies, be brought together to adequately cover the rich and expansive territory that such interdisciplinary work addresses. Indeed, I think it might not be too much to say that African American studies' and other ethnic studies' approaches have pioneered the kind of intellectual work in the academy that is rapidly leading us into what some have termed a postdisciplinary age.

I agree with Spillers that all these developments enable important new kinds of intellectual work. We can hope — and again I quote from her notes — that these new kinds of academic writing "alter an old power dynamic toward a new order of synthesis and inclusion." Indeed, I think they have already begun to do so, and for that I thank the prophetic voice of Hortense Spillers.

REFERENCES

Powell, Malea. 2002. "Listening to Ghosts: An Alternative (Non)Argument." In *ALT DIS: Alternative Discourses in the Academy*, edited by Christopher Schroeder, Helen Fox, and Patricia Bizzell, 11–22. Portsmouth, NH: Heinemann-Boynton/Cook.

Spillers, Hortense. 1985a. "Afterword: Crosscurrents, Discontinuities: Black Women's Fiction." In *Conjuring: Black Women, Fiction, and Literary Tradition*, edited by Marjorie Pryse and Hortense Spillers, 249–61. Bloomington: Indiana University Press.

Spillers, Hortense. 1985b. "Chosen Place, Timeless People: Some Figurations on the New World." In *Conjuring: Black Women, Fiction, and Literary Tradition*, edited by Marjorie Pryse and Hortense Spillers, 151–75. Bloomington: Indiana University Press.

Spillers, Hortense, and Marjorie Pryse, eds. 1985c. *Conjuring: Black Women, Fiction, and Literary Tradition*. Indianapolis: Indiana University Press.

Weber, Max. 1958. "Science as a Vocation." In *Max Weber: Essays in Sociology*, edited by Hans Heinrich Gerth and Charles Wright Mills, 129–56. New York: Oxford University Press.

MELANIE BENSON TAYLOR

nine Being the Emergency

A Response to Hortense Spillers

I received Hortense Spillers's wonderful title a few weeks ahead of her presentation, so I had some time to ponder that evocative idea, "states of emergency," and wonder whatever could she mean by that? I thought I knew when, about a week ago, I experienced my own personal state of emergency: the clock was ticking down toward this sensational occasion that we'd been planning and anticipating for so long, and I hadn't yet committed a single word to paper (and at the same time, I was consumed with teaching two literature classes with over a hundred students who were writing a lot more than I was). Yes, I nearly hit the proverbial panic button. But this sort of crisis is actually fairly routine in the academy, and it pales beside the reality of actual disasters worthy of Spillers's metaphor. Indeed, the kind of emergency she writes of is not a metaphor at all, but an irrefutably real, systemic, and ceaseless condition of urgency and fear that underlies the work we do in our respective fields. It would be exceptionally easy for me to simply echo everything that Spillers has shared with us, to affirm how potently this phenomenon attends my own practice in Native American studies. But rather than reiterate her points, I want to derive two crucial lessons from them: first, a recognition of the stunted promises of interdisciplinarity, which in practice has often yielded more parochialism than collaboration and has often inhibited the kind of rich, kindred, cross-cultural, and disciplinary dialogue that we are enacting here. That brings me to my second point, which is that we need reminders now more than ever of the power of such conversations, embodied and sustained in flagrant acts of rhetorical audacity, because the obstacles we thought we had surmounted tend to reinvent themselves everywhere we go, in both hostile and friendly territory. Native American, African American, and all other minority or interdisciplinary studies programs exist primarily to redress historical exclusions and erasures, but we are deceptively adroit at reinstating old structures of separatism and untenable essentialisms in the guise of innovation (perhaps we've just been too well conditioned . . .). So there is more involved in the perilous call to *write* than simply managing the fraught lives and discourses we were born into; we must also ward off the doppelgängers of suppression that we impose on ourselves. In all of this, we are required to be active agents of both destruction *and* reconstruction. My husband recently reminded me (when I was wandering around the house musing on "states of emergency" and looking pointedly at piles of student essays and laundry) that "states of emergency" are invoked precisely when our usual methods for maintaining order fail, and troops and special dispensations are brought in to mitigate the disaster at all costs. In these moments of crisis and redemption, we are not just the task force — we must, first and foremost, *be* the emergency itself. We are both the disaster and the relief; both the hurricane and the agencies commissioned to rebuild after it.

It would be tempting to say that writing is merely the instrument or the medium for these ideals of collaboration and justice, particularly in a world that values concrete, material measures over the seductive abstractness of the written word. I will admit to periodic bouts of anxiety about this myself, especially in Native American studies, with colleagues from more practical disciplines who spend weeks and months studying and effecting real political, economic, educational, and legal change in tribal communities. I am a literary critic, and the compass of my pen can feel guiltily small in comparison. But we have to believe that writing can effect positive change in our communities precisely because it has long proven its capacity to do just the opposite. Perhaps the most vital contribution Spillers has made — long before her remarks here — was her now-famous essay, "Mama's Baby, Papa's Maybe." In that essay, she described the minority experience in America as a trauma not just in the flesh but in the word. As she put it, there is an oppressive "American grammar" that violently constructs and constricts black female subjectivity, rendering it "a meeting ground of investments and privations in the national treasury of rhetorical wealth. My country needs me, and if I were not here, I would have to be invented" (1987, 65). So many of us who have been marginalized by race, culture, gender, and sexuality found our own experiences described in Spillers's luminous prose and haunting insights. Certainly, this phenomenon of rhetorical violence also describes the invention of the "Indian," a word that supplanted and totalized a preexisting, heteroglot collection of tribes — and, in doing so, utterly transformed not just our lexicons but our lives. When women like Spillers and I participate in any academic or social discourse, we enter contested rhetorical spaces that presume to know us and that depend on our ontological stability, on our willingness to toe the proverbial yet perilous line. The danger in all of this is that we often overestimate our power, assuming that if it is just words, then we can outwit them, but in doing do, we dramatically underestimate just how potent those words can be. Equally deceptive are the moments when we *think* we are performing revolutionary acts of revision but are instead simply recreating new prisons of absolute difference and essentialism. This happens routinely in Native American studies, where so much of what we create resembles a fun house of mainstream mirrors, costumes, and tropes, skewed in playful and parodic postures but nonetheless intact. America "needs" the Indian, just as it needed and invented its African American others; but Indian Country needs Indians, too, and the difference is often one of semantics more than substance.

That seems to be the primary pitfall of our interdisciplinary programs, which often forfeit their transcendent potential in favor of nation building — a worthy enterprise, and a vital one for indigenous nations. We erect our own silos in the academy, just a little more homespun and weather-beaten than the older, ivory prototypes next door. Worse still, we create barriers *within* our own departments to safeguard disciplinary or theoretical turf — silos within silos, if you will. This is not just institutional entropy, of course, but the allure of intellectual solidarity and the cradle of culture that we need to sustain our energies. But if that's all we do, then we have failed to achieve our potential. Although true interdisciplinarity may entail uncomfortable juxtapositions and unexpected collisions, this is the real, complicated, if scarred home territory that we must work from in order to ensure that both our private articulations and our collective narratives are appropriately plural, relational, and authentic. In the end, what we say matters less than the fact that we are speaking for ourselves at all, and that we dare to do so in new ways and contexts, even if we have to muddle through disorientiation and despair along the way. Like William Faulkner's Benjy Compson, the idiot narrator of *The Sound and the Fury*, we are "trying to say" ([1929] 2011, 53) and attempting to give voice to the often ineffable trauma and grief that can structure and stymie our consciousness, lock us into our own echo chambers of loss. In our fields, if we simply "try to say" what it is that haunts us, undoubtedly, someone will hear us.

I deliberately quoted Faulkner here instead of, say, Toni Morrison or Louise Erdrich. That's because both Spillers and I have devoted quite a bit of critical attention to this white male writer from Mississippi, certainly more than anyone might expect us to. But these are reciprocal moves that Faulkner probably would have appreciated, given how deeply he was influenced by the former slaves and the Indian ghosts in his haunted southern cosmos. Because my primary field is southern studies, I am always attuned to the ways that seemingly distinct groups — like white neo-aristocrats and their indigenous neighbors — actually echo one another across fences and water fountains about matters of loss, tradition, community, ecology, and purity. No one expects me to bring Faulkner into the Native American studies classroom, I'm sure, but I do — along with films like *The Shining* and the work of the contemporary Slovenian theorist Slavoj Žižek. And I think — I'm going to go out on a limb here — I *think* this is why the classes I teach here under the rubric of Native American studies tend to have a startling amount of appeal and enrollments from across the campus. It's because students quickly discover that the "Indian" texts and issues we study expose far more encompassing and contemporary crises of agency, value, and justice for *all* human subjects. I ask my students to excavate issues that are in fact deeply personal, entangled with indigenous epistemes but often forcibly alienated from them. Often, I'll let them choose creative writing projects that invite them to fashion their own narratives in response to the ones we're reading, and they're often astonished to discover just how much they have to say, how many parallel (and perpendicular) narratives exist within them. Perhaps most unnerving — for all of us — is the class I am teaching right now, called "Indian Killers" — which is not about colonial removal or genocide per se, but about how those histories haunt us all in this contemporary world of ours, where we continue to dispossess, attack, and retaliate against each other for material advantage and power. We confront the realization that terrible

violence pervades all of our lives in ways that we fail to appre-
hend, because it is silent or systemic, historical or remote, symbolic or rhetorical. These revelations can be uncomfortable, to
say the least; but, as the magnificent Mississippi Choctaw writer
Louis Owens once said, "Literary terrorism is preferable to literary tourism" (1998, 46). These rhetorical acts can be frightening,
but in the end, they are far better than the quiet terror of being
surveilled and spoken *for* in the national museum of American
stereotypes and mythologies.

I appreciate Spillers's contribution so much because although
she acknowledges the sense of community and collaboration that
are integral to our work as minority and interdisciplinary scholars,
she is also unapologetic about the fact that writing is, at bottom, a
deeply intimate vocation. Rarely in academic work are we invited
to wax autobiographical; it seems somehow indulgent or narcis-
sistic, certainly not scholarly in any traditional way. But this is a
vital part of the apparatus of defiance that Spillers is endorsing
here, and it has always struck me as profoundly strange to deny or
excuse the most personal acts of articulation, even and especially
as they wend their way into our cultural and academic communities. If we repudiate that nexus of the personal and the political,
then we dehumanize everything we are called and committed
to do in the academy. So I want to end on a personal note, because it seems crucial to acknowledge that I would not be here
today — a professor at an Ivy League college, in the company
of such esteemed colleagues, quoting improbable mentors like
Faulkner and Spillers — I could not be here if I hadn't first radically revised the script underwriting my life: my socioeconomic
prologue, as it were. My story may not be unique in America, but
neither is it a typical academic biography. I was born into a long
line of blue-collar Indians and Italians in a working-class tourist
economy on Cape Cod. No one in my extended family had ever

been to college, never mind anything beyond, and few people ever left the cape at all. But when I started walking around the house with an issue of *Reader's Digest* tucked under my arm at the age of three, it quickly seemed impossible that I wouldn't do all of those things and more. My mother was a house cleaner, and while she scrubbed rich peoples' bathtubs, I would scour the contents of their bookshelves; while she washed and ironed and hung curtains in their windows, I wrote elaborate stories about imaginary dramas behind those panes of glass. So much of what we've talked about here has entailed defying the rules, but first I absorbed them wholesale: I won grammar contests and spelling bees; I taught myself Latin in grade school and mastered it in college. I simply fell in love with the power of language and devoured it entirely. I internalized everything that constituted raw material for my journey, and once I was full of the timbers and templates and phonemes, I began the arduous but exhilarating process of crafting my entry into an academic environment that seemed (and probably always will seem) alien, terrifying, and strange. It was expensive, exhausting, and at times humiliating, and I can count on perhaps the fingers of one hand the number of times I ever spoke in any of my undergraduate or graduate classes combined (much to my students' disbelief and dismay now). But as long as I had books and writing to retreat to, to help me identify and articulate the vast inequities and the hurt that my experience only grazed, I somehow felt at home. In the disparate multiethnic and regional literatures that I studied, I discovered echoes of my own life in remote geographical and cultural iterations I could never have imagined; and through the sometimes obstinate multidisciplinary course that I charted along the way, I learned that I could engineer my own place here, and not simply occupy the office chair and destiny that some other scholar before me had warmed (at least, they gave me tenure, so I think it's okay!). I remember vividly that when I first got the offer to join the Native American studies program here, one of my new colleagues called to welcome me. He said, "You're a perfect example of someone who *wrote* her way into a better job." What he meant, I knew, in the best possible way, is that I lacked the usual Ivy League pedigree (well, any pedigree at all): in graduate school and my first jobs at mid-tier institutions, I had continued to haunt the margins of something better; I thought I was relegated permanently to the nosebleed section of higher education and of higher everything. But all the while, I did what I had always done when I was on the periphery of elite lives and mansions: I wrote my way in. And in doing so, I altered not just my own narrative, but — I can only hope — those of the students I've had the privilege of shepherding along the way, arming them with both grammar and gumption; and of the writers whose worlds I visited; and of the conversations and canons I shook them out of or into.

Of all the reconfigurations of knowledge in which I have been privileged to participate, though, I am perhaps most proud of this opportunity here — this chance to share the stage and the conversation with a scholar whose work I admire deeply, whose words have repeatedly spoken to and shaped me over the years and miles, and to enact in our dialogue this extraordinarily personal yet incredibly communal power of writing. In this case, we are not just word and metaphor but flesh and voice as well, and that is a profoundly assertive and auspicious turnabout in our histories of ventriloquism and erasure. In our world of continued privations, exclusions, poverty, and injustice, we *are always already* in a state of emergency. But those of us in interdisciplinary studies — and, really, in the liberal arts environment more broadly — are uniquely poised to rise collectively above the borders of race, class, discipline, and every other orientation that we have let divide and conquer us.

So I want to affirm Spillers's buoyancy, and I want to do so in an appropriately rhetorical revision. Because I am a Latinist, and because I love to play with words, I want to change the metaphor that we have been testing here. I want to let loose from the word "emergency" its sister term "emergence," which comes from the same Latin root, meaning to emerge, to rise up or out, to bring to light. That is what we do when we write our way up and out in this world, when we bring to light experiences concealed in the rubble of national amnesia and invention. We may not change the world with every paper or book we write, but every word changes us, slowly but surely — and when the time is right and emergencies rock the ground beneath us, *we* are the words that both shatter and deliver us.

REFERENCES

Faulkner, William. (1929) 2011. *The Sound and the Fury*. New York: Random House.

Owens, Louis. 1998. "Multicultural Tourism: Native American Literature, Canon, and Campus." In Louis Owens, *Mixedblood Messages: Literature, Film, Family, Place*, 42-47. Norman: University of Oklahoma Press.

Spillers, Hortense J. 1987. "Mama's Baby, Papa's Maybe: An American Grammar Book." *Diacritics* 17, no. 2: 64-81.

part 4 Humanities

KATHERINE BERGERON

ten Listening to Write

I want to thank Christiane Donahue for organizing this wonderful project and for offering me the opportunity to reflect on the important role of writing in my own academic career. I should begin by saying that I originally misunderstood the invitation that Christiane sent me requesting my participation. At the time I received it, I was serving as the dean of the college at Brown University, and in that role I had worked strategically to strengthen the undergraduate writing requirement. So when I opened the e-mail message, I naturally thought I was being asked to speak from this perspective: to talk about the importance of writing for a liberal education. But my work in administration accounts for only part of my identity. I am also a musicologist who has written extensively about French music and poetry around the beginning of the twentieth century. And it was only on a second reading of Christiane's invitation that I realized I was, in fact, being asked to address that career. What has it meant for me to be a writer in my own discipline, and how have I handled the task of writing about an art as elusive as music?

The questions are both intriguing and challenging: intriguing, because it is always instructive to reflect on one's own habits; challenging, because this kind of scrutiny can easily become solipsistic. When we talk about writing we mean, of course, writing about something. But if the something is one's own writing process, the result might begin to appear like the effect the French call a *mise en abîme*: a reflection that reaches toward a point of no return. I will try to avoid that result here by frequently changing my angle on the question — alternating passages of self-scrutiny with close readings of music and poetry — and by shifting the idea of reflection itself from the visual to the aural realm, from looking to listening. What I hope to demonstrate in this essay, through a series of observations and musical examples, are two lessons I have learned again and again in the course of my career as a musicologist: how writing about music can teach you to listen more deeply; and how listening can show you a different way to write.

Invention

Let me start with a confession. For some reason, when I write, I always have to begin at the beginning. Every book I have written began with the first sentence of the first chapter. I did not get very far with this talk today, in fact, until I had started writing the first paragraph. Writing, for me, means beginning. Oh, there are all kinds of things I do to get going before I start: coming up with a title, jotting down thoughts, making lists. For me, though, that is not exactly writing. When I am writing I am compelled to bring order to those jottings, and that requires, in turn, both having an idea of what I want to say and then beginning to say it. For the writer, then, the real question becomes: What does it take to have an idea? That is the first topic I want to explore here.

Music, as it turns out, offers an interesting angle on that question. And so as my first example, I want to begin where music scholars frequently begin: by turning to Johann Sebastian Bach. I am thinking specifically of a book of fifteen short keyboard pieces that Bach brought out in 1723. The manuscript advertised that it was a manual of "straightforward instruction" and went on to say that the pieces would make students not only better players but also better composers by showing them, in Bach's terms, how to "get good inventions."[1] (That is how he put it. We now refer to this collection as the *Two-Part Inventions* because Bach labeled each piece with the Latin term *inventio*. Perhaps also for this reason, we tend to think of a Bach invention as a kind of musical form, like a sonata or a minuet, but that does not seem to have been the original intent. As Bach saw them, the inventions were a means to an end, a way for a student to "get good inventions." To put it in terms that are relevant to this book, they were pieces designed to show what it takes to write well — in short, to have a good idea — on the keyboard.

Interestingly, this also seems to be what the term *inventio* meant in classical rhetoric. One of Cicero's earliest writings on rhetoric bore the title *De inventione* (On the inventions). It was a book intended for speakers in the law courts, offering detailed accounts of the kinds of arguments and strategies necessary for making a plausible case. The inventions had to do with topics suitable for argument, or the general sources of argument, but in Cicero's account they were not so much themes as procedures: partitioning, conjugating, contradicting, comparing, and so on. They were, in other words, the steps one needed to take to develop a good idea. This is no less true today, for how can you make a good case without understanding it in all its parts, definitions, contradictions, and analogies? In other words, you cannot have a good idea until you actually *have* the idea. Invention refers to the extent of this intellectual embrace: the whole matrix of logical relations that someone skilled in argument ought to have worked out.

In Cicero's time, those skilled practitioners were orators rather than writers. And for Bach, of course, they were keyboard players. How, then, does this concept of invention play out on the keyboard? As a musicologist, I could answer in two possible ways. I could, for example, simply look at a score. There I could see all the contrapuntal strategies that Bach uses to spin out the invention: the countersubjects, transpositions, imitations, sequences,

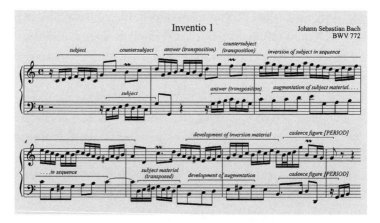

FIGURE 10.1 Contrapuntal analysis of Johann Sebastian Bach's
Invention in C major, BWV 772.

inversions, augmentations, and other techniques that were the
common practice in his day (figure 10.1). This kind of visual accounting is useful, and it functions, in a way, like Cicero's treat-
ment of the inventions: as a table, or a list, of possible permuta-
tions. Another way to grasp the invention, of course, would be
to listen to it. Listening to a performance, in fact, often exposes
things that a score cannot show. This is a very basic but critical point. In the case of the C Major Invention, there are many
performances to choose from. I recommend a recording by the
Canadian pianist Angela Hewitt, from her DVD *Bach Performance
at the Piano* (2008), which has a character and verve that I find
compelling.

When you listen, you will note that the piece lasts barely a
minute. This tightly wound little invention is over before we know
it, suggesting that the music is meant to do a different kind of
work. Like a diagram in a book, it is a piece for study. The kind
of study Bach had in mind was not so much visual as physical,
taking place, as it did, at the keyboard. Players were meant to

explode the diagram manually by working through its parts step by step. They would, in a very literal sense, learn to handle the various contrapuntal operations by getting these strategies under their fingers. Or, to put it again in terms relevant to this book, players could understand the invention — what it means to have a musical idea — by feeling their way through it, learning to "write" the counterpoint with their hands. We shouldn't forget, after all, that *inventio* (from the Latin *invenire*) means discovery.

Slow Listening

This is a discovery I make, in any case, from listening to the invention rather than merely looking at it. And here, then, lies the bigger challenge for the musicologist: Is it possible to write about that kind of writing, about the embodied experience of a performance? That's a question that has motivated my own work over the past two decades, and it's worth staying with the invention just a bit longer to see how we might address it in this context. So I want to go back now and listen again — this time, just to the opening measures. The music represented in figure 10.1 amounts to what we might call the first period. That is a rhetorical term, too, referring to a complete thought, but, again, I am less interested in the terms than in the quality of the musical movement that governs this *inventio*, this musical idea. So how does this invention move? Well, just as we might expect a little piece in C major to move: with a lot of naïve enthusiasm. The right hand, for example, jumps into action before it's quite ready. Barely pausing for a breath, it races up the white keys toward G, falls back, then springs ahead in a quick rebound to G and to the octave, where it bounces in place until restarting the race on higher ground. Meanwhile, from below, the left hand has been imitating this playful movement at a distance — rushing forward with the leaps, and leaping with the runs — until it reaches the point where the right hand began. Here, from this new perch, the two partners lock elbows in preparation for an exuberant downward tumble that comes to a temporary rest in a new place: the dominant key of G.

What has this narrative account done for us? For one thing, it is intentionally active, the prose description relying heavily on verbs that will convey the quality of the movement: racing, springing, bouncing, tumbling. These are not verbs I would choose, for example, to convey the melancholy second invention in C minor. But the prose is also quite deliberate, especially in its effort to catch hold of an action that took place in just twenty seconds. In my book *Voice Lessons*, I refer to that deliberateness as "slow listening" (2010, xiv). I could have called it "close reading," but I was looking for a term that captured both the aural and the temporal aspects of the listening experience. And as I said in the book, I was also trying to find a way of writing that would make the sound more clearly felt. This requires close attention to the affective and expressive qualities of language — not just its register, but also its tempo and diction — in order to approximate the experience of something that does, after all, take place in time. Of course, it also takes time to capture the quality of movement, which is partly what I mean by "slow" listening. Expressed through prose, the listening encounter becomes like a slow-motion replay, lingering over the details so we can grasp them more intimately. In fact, if I were to read aloud my description of that passage, it would take twice as long to hear than to play the musical excerpt it refers to.

And what do we gain from this lingering? In short, an ability to hear more. The effect is like blowing up a photographic image, or listening through a stethoscope. But it is more than a technical operation. The imaginative, or poetic, dimension of writing affords me a different kind of access to the music, allowing me to find my way *inside* the musical line. And from the perspective of this new place, I feel a new responsibility, like that of a translator, to articulate what the music is saying about itself. This, of course, produces a different kind of writing, one that bends language to meet its object. Baudelaire once famously described the poet as a translator, and it's fair to say that the kind of translation I am talking about takes inspiration from poetry. In any case, it is a different way to get at what it means to have an idea in music, and the difference is key, for it helps to signal that something else is going on: a kind of listening that makes the music present. Let's call this kind of writing a *listening from within*. I like to think of it more basically as a performance — a writing that honors the embodied nature of music by conveying its character through a performance of language.

Performing Language

I want to explore this mode of performative listening in the remainder of this essay by turning to two more examples drawn from my book *Voice Lessons*. The first involves listening *into* the voice of a particular performer, a famous singer from the past; the second involves listening to the voice of a poem. In each case, as I hope to show, the effort to get inside these voices leads to some surprising discoveries, which, in turn, bring forth new and more sympathetic modes of writing.

Voice Lessons is an unusual history of an unusual repertory: the late-blooming art of song known as *la mélodie française*, or French melody. In the book I try to tell the story of that art from the point of view not just of its music and poetry but also of its performances: the voices that animated the sound of both. I hardly need to say that a voice, like a color or a sound, is a difficult thing to write about. The French critic Roland Barthes once complained about this difficulty in a well-known essay, "The Grain of the Voice," chiding music criticism for relying too heavily, as he put it, on "the poorest of linguistic categories, the adjective" (1985, 179). He called for an alternative writing in which music would escape this status of a weak predicate and meet language head on, and he called that encounter the "grain."

What I am calling a *listening from within* is akin to Barthes's idea of the grain, I think, because it recognizes the productive friction of the writer's intervention. In *Voice Lessons*, I was all the more eager to get this intervention right because the music I was studying was already self-conscious about its relationship to writing. The melodies of Gabriel Fauré, Claude Debussy, and other composers of their generation were as aware of the writing of poets as the poems of Paul Verlaine and Stéphane Mallarmé were aware of song. In short, I needed a new kind of listening simply to gain access to my historical subject: a body of music and poetry that was all *about* the performance of language.

This self-consciousness is particularly audible in the voices of singers who performed the music best. One such performer was Claire Croiza, who sang with Fauré and Debussy in Paris during the years around World War I and, fortunately for us, took the trouble to record some of her performances for posterity. The recordings she made in the late 1920s, at the height of her fame, offer the most literal type of sound writing we have, giving us direct access to the repertory of French *mélodie*. But these, too, require a different kind of listening. A voice preserved from the distant past — like an image preserved in an old photograph — can seem strange because its manner is so different from what we know, but if we learn to listen into that difference, other values come into view, offering important lessons of their own. Croiza made a much admired recording for Columbia in 1927 that can teach us a great deal. It is her interpretation of the "letter scene" from Act I of Debussy's *Pelléas et Mélisande*, and it is worth spending some time to listen closely to her interpretation.[2] Croiza plays the role of Geneviève, the mother of the two half-brothers, Pelléas and Golaud. In the scene, Geneviève reads aloud a letter that Golaud has written to Pelléas explaining his encounter with a mysterious, crying girl named Mélisande who has just as mysteriously become his bride. Here is what Geneviève sings as the curtain opens:

Voici ce qu'il écrit à son frère Pelléas:
"Un soir, je l'ai trouvée tout en pleurs au bord d'une fontaine
Dans la forêt où je m'étais perdue.
Je ne sais ni son âge, ni qui elle est, ni d'où elle vient, et je n'ose
    pas l'interroger,
Car elle doit avoir eu une grande épouvante, et quand on lui de-
    mande ce qui lui est arrivé,
Elle pleure tout à coup comme un enfant et sanglote,
Si profondément qu'on a peur."

("Here is what he has written to his brother Pelléas: 'One evening, I found her sobbing at the banks of a spring in the forest where I had become lost. I do not know how old she is, nor who she is, nor where she comes from, and I dare not ask. For she must have had some terrible fright, and when you ask her what happened, she bursts into tears like a child and sobs so deeply that it frightens you.'")

One of the most striking — and strange — aspects of Croiza's performance of this "letter scene" is the quality of her diction. The balance of word to tone in her singing seems to have shifted to place more weight onto the word, even onto individual letters. She is reading *writing*, after all. Croiza's singing makes the context clear, the monotone line suggesting what it feels like to read someone else's words aloud.

But the diction makes some other values clear as well. There is deliberateness in Croiza's declamation, a deliberateness that is worth attending to closely. It is apparent in the way she renders every consonant and vowel, and especially her handling of that uniquely French sound known as *l'e muet*, the mute *e*. This is a syllable that disappears in everyday speech but gains clarity and purpose in formal French address. Its neutral timbre is almost as difficult to describe as to pronounce, constituting one of the major differences between French and the other European languages. If you try to find the sound inside a French mouth, you discover that it has an unusual profile: located at the dead center of the tongue, it is has neither the somber quality of a front vowel or the brightness of a back vowel but rather the dull gray color of something that sits exactly in the middle: ə. A French linguist from the period of *Pelléas* once described it as a supremely empty phoneme: the sound French people make when they open their mouths and have nothing to say.

The unique color of this vowel is audible in Croiza's declamation, but if we listen even more closely we begin to recognize that this apparently mute syllable carries more expressive weight than we first thought. Indeed, if we slow her performance down further, we can hear not only how this syllable becomes longer or shorter according to its place in the declamation, but also how it shows up in places we don't expect — slipped in like a shim, for instance, between two consonants to give them more room. For example, instead of saying simply "Un soir, je l'ai trouvée tout en pleurs au bord d'une fontaine," she says "Un soir(e), je l'ai t(e) rou-vée tout en p(e)leurs au bor(e) d'un-e fon-tai-ne." In other words, she adds in more of the silent syllables to emphasize the consonants. And she does a similar thing later on when reading a line about Mélisande's sudden bouts of tears: "Elle pleure tout à coup comme un enfant et sanglote si profondément qu'on a

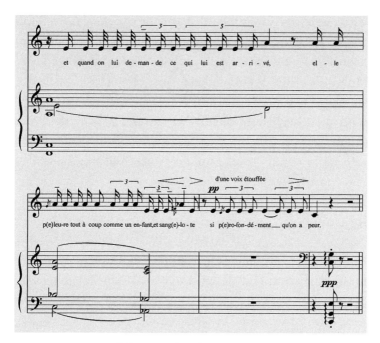

FIGURE 10.2 Notation of Claire Croiza's performance of Act I, scene 2, *Pelléas et Mélisande*, by Claude Debussy. The grace notes indicate where Croiza has embellished the melodic line through her pronunciation.

peur." Croiza sings: "Ell-e p(e)leur-e tout à coup comme un enfant et san-g(e)lo-te si p(e)ro-fon-dé-ment qu'on a peur." Here the slipped-in syllables are treated even more boldly, turned into melodic embellishments — lower neighbors or passing tones — of the existing monotone line (figure 10.2).

So where is this deep listening headed? Have I, like Golaud, become lost in a forest of symbols? Not quite. I do feel a bit like a detective, though, inspecting the grainy evidence of an enlarged surveillance photo to see the drama that has just taken place. Blowing up the detail allows me to enter that drama — the encounter of music and language that produces the mute *e*'s telling behavior. From this privileged interior perspective I can see, in fact, how the *e* serves to clarify the liquid *l* phoneme in the words *pleure* and *sanglote*, as if to bring out the liquidity of Mélisande's tears. Yet in another sense, nothing has happened at all. The muted interventions are *im*pressions rather than *ex*pressions, designed to keep emotion on the inside. What this drama of letters exposes, then, is a very different expressive culture, one with a scale of values tipped toward silence. And only this kind of close-up listening gives me access to it.

Poetic Inventions

With this hushed drama of letters still in our ears, I want to turn to one final example. This time I will discuss a poem rather than a piece of music, to see how the poets in the era of the *mélodie* were themselves moved by language's silent brush with music. I have chosen a poem, in fact, by one figure from this period who made this encounter central to his aesthetic, one who saw the pure idea of poetry in the "near vibratory disappearance" of language, as he famously put it. I am speaking, of course, of Mallarmé. Listening slowly and intimately to one of Mallarmé's poems should allow us hear our way into those muted vibrations. But, as with Geneviève's scene of reading, we will also discover that there is more resonating there than we first expected.

The poem I have chosen is called "Eventail" (Fan), and it is a little verse that Mallarmé wrote on the surface of a Japanese paper fan as a gift for his daughter:

O rêveuse, pour que je plonge
Au pur délice sans chemin
Sache, par un subtil mensonge,
Garder mon aile dans ta main.

Une fraîcheur de crepuscule
Te vient à chaque battement
Dont le coup prisonnier recule
L'horizon délicatement.

Vertige! Voici que frisonne
L'espace comme un grand baiser
Qui, fou de naître pour personne
Ne peut jaillir ni s'apaiser.

Sens-tu le paradis farouche
Ainsi qu'un rire enseveli
Se couler du coin de ta bouche
Au fond de l'unanime pli!

Le sceptre des rivages roses
Stagnants sur les soirs d'or, ce l'est
Ce blanc vol fermé que tu poses
Contre le feu d'un bracelet. (1998, 83)

("O dreamer girl, so that I might plunge/ Into pure, directionless delight,/ Learn, by a subtle lie,/ To keep my wing in your hand.// A twilight freshness/ Comes to you with each beat/ Whose captive gust/ Delicately pushes back the horizon// I swoon! See how the space trembles/ Like a great, wild kiss, / which, born for no one in particular,/ Can neither erupt nor abate.// Don't you feel the savage paradise — /As you might a stifled laugh/ Flowing from the corner of your mouth — /At the heart of the unanimous fold!// The scepter of stagnant pink shores/ On top of golden evenings: this is it,/ This closed white wing that you place/ Against a bracelet's fire.//")

The first thing to note in reading the poem aloud is, of course, the sound of the verse. The unrelenting stream of sibilants serves to convey a sense of the captive gusts — the more or less silent movement of the air — that constitute one of the poem's central conceits. This is, after all, a poem about a fan. But it is also a poem in a fan, or at least on a fan, that Mallarmé presented as a gift. So as soon as the reading starts, we are dealing with at least three points of view. There is the fan, the material poem, which is also a subject of the poem. There is the person who opens the fan, the poem's reader. And there is the person who has given the fan away, the poem's writer, who may seem to speak through the fan, but who ultimately remains absent. No wonder the poem swoons.

1. The fan speaks first. It asks to be held and opened so that it can experience the pleasure of being moved. From the fan's perspective, this is a little like flying, plunging "into pure directionless delight." But it is like lying, too, because the fan doesn't really take off. It's stuck — like the poem, perhaps — between words on the wing (a tired cliché), and the wing in the wind (a bit more fun: éventail actually has a trace of both words, *vent* and *aile*, wrapped within it). So the poem makes a deal.

2. This is what you'll get, it says, by doing as I ask. By moving me, a delicious *coup de vent* — a breath of fresh air — will be moved back toward you. And with its rhyming eight-syllable lines, like a sweet *chanson*, the poem is already an air, of sorts. And so a question arises: Who or what is doing the moving? Is the fan moving the air, or is the air actually moving the fan? Thinking through the puzzle can make you dizzy, but that vertigo is just another a pun — *vertige* formed from the word for poem (*vers*) and the word for stem (*tige*). The collision causes the question to disappear again into the folded form that fans out, like a flower, from the dreamer's clutch.

3. Now we are at the middle of the poem. And here, on the

other side of the exclamation point, the perspective shifts. The punctuation, it seems, has set this space (and its air) atremble, and that changes the stakes. Whatever deal we made before apparently no longer belongs to just you and me. The pleasure now lies somewhere in between, like an air kiss proffered to no one. This opening of the playing field leads to more pleasure, and another question.

4. Don't you feel that wildness growing inside you, like laughter that just has to get out? It seems that the fan is now being questioned. But who is asking? Is it the air? the girl? Or have we moved to that space on the other side, where the absent author sits?

5. Ah, yes, *this* is it. Or so the omniscient last stanza announces, remembering the pretty scene painted on the paper front — a sunset, an oriental shore. But now those folds are closed for good, lain to rest on a pretty wrist where just a bracelet shines.

I will admit that, even after years of reading this poem, its difficulties are still palpable; but so, too, are its pleasures. The sense of plunging into pure directionless delight is something that the poem promises — and that I can look forward to — each time I open it. This is one way, perhaps, that reading the poem is like listening to music. For you can't really have this poem *except* in the act of performing it; and that involves not only attending to the multiple voices but also following the figures as they spin out — fan out — in many directions and many dimensions at once: splitting, recombining, rhyming, connecting, conjugating, mirroring, doubling back. What I'm describing, in fact, is not so different from what I described at the beginning of this essay when glossing the experience of a Bach invention. It's like writing counterpoint on a keyboard: the whole, complex network of relations shows you, in very real terms, the meaning of *inventio*, discovery — what it means to have an idea.

Listening to Write

Which brings me back to writing, and to two final points. I suppose there is some poetic justice in ending this essay on writing about music writing with a poet whose own *oeuvre* embraced the same issues and the same kind of reflexivity. Mallarmé opens our ears to the remarkable polyphony of thought that makes up an act of writing. And it is precisely that texture that I want to catch in my own writing — my own performances, you could say — as a music critic. I have summarized this critical activity as different forms of *listening*. But there is one type of listening that I haven't yet mentioned — one that is just as essential to my writing process. I'm speaking about listening to my own prose: yes, that's right — reading my writing aloud.

Writing, like music, is an art of time. When you take the time to read aloud, you change your relationship to what you have written. You become audience to your own thought, grasping its contours in new ways. Listening to your writing allows you to rehearse like a performer — testing your interpretation, shifting the tone, adjusting tempo and rhythm — to bring out the character of your ideas, to get the thinking right. It moves the text from the state of a past participle ("something written") to the present progressive ("something I am attending to"). Most importantly, like the other kinds of listening I have discussed, it makes *you* present.

Why is this so important? That's the final thing I want to address. Indeed — at a moment when the value of the humanities is being questioned not only in the public sphere but in our universities — it seems all the more important to say, in a very public way, why the kind of writing process I have been discussing matters. In this essay I have tried to show what it means to write about an art as elusive as music. That work, for me, has been all about making experience present, reaching across a space of difference to get inside a work from the past, to hear what it is saying about itself. It's not the easiest thing to do, but it has some important ancillary benefits. It teaches you to scrutinize your perceptions and, more critically, to hear and empathize with voices that are different from your own. If you spend your life doing that, you develop capacities for understanding that are not only central to the humanities; they are also exactly what we believe every liberally educated citizen should have. You could call it the ability to translate across difference. I might call it, more simply, compassion. And I daresay there has never been a time in our world when we needed that more.

NOTES

1. The words "Auffrichtige Anleitung" (straightforward instruction) are found at the beginning of Bach's autograph manuscript of the inventions, now housed in the Staatsbibliothek in Berlin. The phrase appears at the top of the opening page as a kind of title.

2. The recording I discuss here can be found on *Claire Croiza: Champion of the Modern French Mélodie*, Marston 52018-2, © 1999. The vagaries of the modern record industry have, unfortunately, made this title extremely hard to find. Those who purchase my book *Voice Lessons* will be able to listen to it through a companion website managed by Oxford University Press.

REFERENCES

Barthes, Roland. 1985. "The Grain of the Voice." In Roland Barthes, *The Responsibility of Forms*, translated by Richard Howard, 179–89. New York: Hill and Wang.

Bergeron, Katherine. 2010. *Voice Lessons: French Mélodie in the Belle Epoque*. New York: Oxford University Press.

Hewitt, Angela. 2008. *Bach Performance at the Piano*. London: Hyperion.

Mallarmé, Stéphane. 1998. *Oeuvres complètes*. Edited by Bertrand Marchal. New ed. Vol. 1. Paris: Gallimard.

MARIA JERSKEY

eleven Writing as a Performance of Language, Listening as an Act of Empathy

A few themes and metaphors emerged during the 2012 Writing Summit at Dartmouth College in connection to writing. Two — voice and music — played beautifully into Katherine Bergeron's vital connection between writing and listening. We can't talk about writing without bringing up voice and music. We notice when words *sing on the page.* We even call the act of writing "composing." Steven Strogatz shared the fact that he listens to his voice to edit his writing — a process he came by intuitively and has since refined, using voice-to-text software. (This isn't a technological innovation per se: Wallace Stevens composed his poems by dictating to his secretary.) David McCullough talked about writing not just for the notes, but to create music. (He also sang a mean version of "Chiquita Banana" at dinner.) In his response to McCullough's remarks, Keith Gilyard reminded us that one of the original Dartmouth Seminar's attendees, James Britton, conceptualized writing as "shaping at the point of utterance" (Britton 1982, 139). Bergeron says that for her, "you cannot have a good idea until you actually *have* the idea." I've loved listening to our keynote speakers share their good ideas about writing. Bergeron sums up much of what's been said during the Writing Summit with her idea of *slow listening.* As a musicologist, she faces in her writing process the challenge of producing a kind of "writing that honors the embodied nature of music by conveying its character through a performance of language."

It's a powerful ability to listen slowly and to translate — from one medium to another — that Bergeron demonstrates in her description of Bach. It takes a powerful ability to teach writing that can do that. As writing teachers, we hope to cultivate a love of writing in our students and, if not a love, at least some faith and confidence in the payoff of McCullough's "good, hard work of writing well." Bergeron's talk reminds us that we also want to cultivate in our students the powerful ability to hear what they've set as their own bar, their own challenge for what they want to accomplish as writers and with their writing. If we've accomplished that much as teachers — cultivating a practice of listening for the voice beyond the words, for the music beyond the notes — then we've accomplished a lot.

The payoff for Bergeron in "making experience present, reaching across a space of difference to get inside a work from the past, to hear what it is saying about itself" is an act of discipline, of hard work, and ultimately of generosity, empathy, and compassion. In describing slow listening, Bergeron observes that "it teaches you to scrutinize your perceptions and, more critically, to hear and empathize with voices that are different from your own. . . . You could call it," she says, "the ability to translate across difference."

I want to riff on that "ability to translate across difference," on Bergeron's contemplation of the empathy and compassion this fosters, and her claim that "there has never been a time in our world when we needed that more." In this she's addressing one of the key questions of the Writing Summit: what is the role of writing in our world today?

Hortense Spillers talked about choosing from among available repertoires and negotiating those repertoires. Her talk of repertoires made me think about language and languages and the struggle to cultivate in ourselves and in our students an awareness of the music of language — even in the academy — that is flexible and creative and goes beyond rigid, unchecked assumptions of linguistic correctness.

One thing we haven't unpacked very much at this summit is the relationship between language — the English language in particular — and writing. In his introduction, Joseph Harris reminded us that the 1966 Dartmouth Seminar was originally called the Anglo-American Conference on the Teaching and Learning of English. He also mentioned the article by our writing studies colleague, John Trimbur, "The Dartmouth Conference and the Geohistory of the Native Speaker" (2008). Trimbur provides a close reading of one aspect of the Dartmouth Seminar: its conceptual framework of the native English speaker. In a discussion that challenges the seminar's "premise of a native speaker" of "linguistic and cultural homogeneity" (144) and the assumption that to teach English, we must love English (164), Trimbur suggests that "rather than assuming affection for English or trying to disseminate it, [perhaps instead we should] explore the ambivalence toward English that has characterized the unsettled linguistic history of the United States" (166).

When I teach linguistics, I feel the unsettled linguistic history of the United States. Even though few of my students at LaGuardia Community College are monolingual English speakers, they are consistently shocked to discover that the United States could be considered anything other than a monolingual country. They can't believe at first that English is not the official language. This assumption goes deep. After all, we talk about teaching writing synonymously with teaching English. I teach what is called ESL writing. I dislike the term ESL. Not only is it more often than not a misnomer — English as a *second* language — but it also carries a not so implicit connotation of deficiency, making my job of cultivating language awareness that much harder. During this Writing Summit, we've talked about math phobia and writing phobia. I can tell you that one of the best ways to cultivate language phobia is by identifying so-called linguistic deficiency. It is so much more productive — and compassionate and creative — to recognize and identify linguistic resources that can shape writing at that delicate, fragile "point of utterance."

Although the idea continues to be hotly debated by people unfamiliar with the studies that prove otherwise, teaching good grammar is still equated with teaching good writing. But can we teach selective notes and still expect music?

I've coauthored three college writing handbooks with my mentor and colleague at the City University of New York, Ann Raimes, who revolutionized how writing handbooks address the needs of multilingual writers. It is still insufficient. I discovered firsthand how challenging it is to go against what Raymond Williams called the "selective tradition" (2001, 68) — that social, cultural, and historical mechanism that selectively chooses out of actual historical periods what will, in fact, be remembered as characteristic — rather than what has actually occurred. Of course, good Marxist that he was, Williams was making the point that the selective tradition typically favors selective groups.

To illustrate the selective tradition's working on British literature in the 1840s, for example, Williams points out that the popular literary purchases at that time ranged from the upper levels of the novel to a "'huge trade' in pornographic books" (2001, 72). In between were publications both racy and sentimental that sold by the thousands, thanks to the new capacity to produce more books for less money, the proliferation of railway stations as venues in which to sell those books, and the commuting from station to station that gave people time and space to read those books. Top-selling titles that are little remembered today like *Agincourt, Last Days of Pompeii, [Mr.] Midshipman Easy, Tower of London, Romance of War* [and] *Scalp Hunters*" (2001, 71) sold as many and, in some cases, even more than works by the giants we remember: Dickens, Thackeray, Austen, or the Brontës. That is, the characteristic authors of the *actual* nineteenth-century British novels are not necessarily the characteristic authors of the nineteenth-century British novels we remember today.

Who chooses what becomes *characteristic?* Why? Who stands to gain? Who stands to lose? What checks and balances might we put into place to demechanize a selective tradition? What is the connection between the selective tradition and how English language usage has been reinscribed in academic milieus?

Consider the innocent college writing handbook, a ubiquitous staple of the college composition classroom and a powerful artifact of a very American preoccupation with correct English usage. Whose *characteristic* English is represented in writing handbooks? And why?

I was fascinated to discover in Bergeron's *Voice Lessons* that, in an effort to secularize its educational system in the nineteenth century, France sought to make the French language "available" to all its citizens. In "rescuing" them from the *patois* and regional dialects and languages that flavored France, officials effectively silenced those languages and varieties in favor of a homogeneous national French voice (Bergeron 2010, 74–75). Their model? The pedagogical methods used by the public school systems in the United States. Both countries have had a history of selecting and promoting one of many languages and equating performances of good grammar (and good *diction*) with moral goodness. This assumption of a relationship between good grammar and moral goodness goes so deeply, it should not be surprising that on very fundamental levels, people feel so strongly about 'good' language.

Music has had its moments of inspiring moral outrage, too. What standards distinguish music from noise? If we think about music in terms of cognitive processes, we can imagine melodies creating synaptic paths that carve grooves into our brains, making it easier for us to take in and retain similar melodies. (Kathleen Yancey's essay implanted Johnny Mathis into my brain for several hours.) But when expectations of familiar melodies (or harmonies or rhythms) are displaced by dissonance or unfamiliar syncopations, we might perceive that our musical grooves have been violated. Is there anything fundamentally wrong with dissonance? Of course not. The magic of music (and of language) is that we build new synaptic paths that make way for new grooves, and it's all pleasure again as dissonance and syncopations convey to us a kind of truth (unless, of course, we resist that truth).

Isn't that what we listen for in the humanities? Don't we appreciate art and music and literature because they resonate — make audible and visible — what's in our hearts? What we tacitly know to be true about the experience of being human? Of being human together? And don't we then use writing as a tool to keep that truth in check? I think we do.

And so language.

We accept others' languages, vernaculars, and dialects in literature — that is, outside of school and outside of scholarship. They have been harder to accept as part of what we teach when we teach writing or assign it in our courses. We need to interrogate that boundary making. To what grooves of language usage do we confine ourselves and our students?

We have historically exalted the native speaker, and now we push for a native-speaker-like proficiency in our students at a great risk: we risk not hearing other ways of knowing, other ways of thinking. We would never have named the 2012 Writing Summit the "Anglo-American Seminar on Writing." In a world where nonnative speakers of English outnumber native speakers three to one (Graddol 1999), we realize that our ideas of English and its relationship to writing need to expand. Addressing issues of linguistic inequity has been fueled by the rapidity of globalization, new media literacies, and critical theoretical perspectives that have called attention to the transcultural flows of people and texts and to the kinds of hybridity and fluidity that characterize language use in the world.

Scholars in writing studies have increasingly critiqued monolingualist assumptions that have governed the ways we talk and write about writing and about our teaching practices. In doing so, we have called for a move toward *translingual writing* (see Horner et al. 2011; Canagarajah 2006). A monolingualist writing paradigm assumes that writers acquire rhetorical competence one language at a time and that what works for English will be different for French or Arabic or Portuguese: there are separate competencies for separate languages. It assumes that texts are informed by rhetorical values that are separate for the different languages in which they are composed, and that only one rhetorical tradition at a time can provide coherence for a text.

One thing that the 1966 Dartmouth Seminar problematized — albeit unintentionally — is that we need to move beyond notions that each language is informed by rhetorical assumptions belonging to a specific culture. English usage in India or South Africa or Texas or Hanover, New Hampshire, is not monolithic. Arabic usage across North Africa and the Middle East is not monolithic. Spanish usage across North America, Latin American, the Caribbean, and Spain is not monolithic.

Writers are not conditioned by their cultures to appreciate only the rhetorical values that they come with. Nor is it difficult for writers to adopt a rhetorical mode that is practiced in a linguistic community other than their own. We're much more flexible as language users. A translingual writing paradigm allows us to address emerging genres of writing whose textual conventions — the complex literacy practices that we see emerging in contemporary social life — go beyond traditional categories. It also invites us to reinvigorate ancient traditions of translingual writing from non-Western communities during precolonial times, traditions that were suppressed during European colonization in favor of a monolingual orientation (see Canagarajah 2006). With translingual writing we have opportunities to move writing toward traditions that predate the monolingual traditions that have served national agendas and certain groups of individuals while disenfranchising others.

Translingual writing is not new to English. Look at Mark Twain's deft integration of vernacular voices across his work. Ken Saro-Wiwa, the Nigerian writer, journalist, and environmental activist, wrote his novel *Sozaboy* in what his first-person narrator called "rotten English" (Saro-Wiwa even subtitled the novel *A Novel in Rotten English*). English may be considered the global lingua franca, but when we look at its use in the world, we see many Englishes. Which one (or ones) do we choose to write in? Why?

When we listen to our own voices (and this reminds me of Gilyard's *Voices of the Self* [1991]), what languages do we hear? What voices do we transcribe? Which voices do we silence? Which ones do we value? Why?

What happens if instead of teaching our students how to write *correct* English — we teach them to choose among their repertoires of languages the language (or dialect or vernacular) that best suits their purpose? What happens if we cultivate linguistic awareness alongside the rhetorical sensitivity and writing strategies that we teach our students to practice? This would allow writing to be a shaping at the point of utterance. This would allow for a slow listening — to our own writing and voices and the writing of others and their voices. It would cultivate Bergeron's "ability to translate across difference."

Does academic writing need to be in Standard Written English? We talk about an increasingly diverse, nontraditional student body; that student body is quickly becoming our faculty. Melanie Benson Taylor observed in her essay that she was the first person in her family to go to college, and here she is teaching at Dartmouth. My colleagues at the City University of New York are from all over the world. Their diversity mirrors our student population's diversity. As we discover and define what it means to live together in a globalized world, it behooves us to recognize and plumb the rich linguistic heritage already present in our academic communities by listening slowly to the voices in translingual writing.

This may be as pragmatically challenging as it is ideologically compelling (if it is ideologically compelling!). When we move toward a translingual practice of academic writing, we move toward uncharted ground. Even as we begin to integrate translingual writing practices into our classes, we grapple with issues that emerge and need to be resolved in our academic settings from the pedagogical and the programmatic to the personal (see Canagarajah 2011).

Does translingual writing need to be taught or just practiced? Is there a place for error or mistakes? How do we assess that? Although we might encourage translingual writing practices in low-stakes activities, how would we integrate those practices into high-stakes writing activities in which students' writing performance is assessed? (Writing assessment, after all, is a big industry.)

How do our student writers relate to translingual writing? What place, for example, is there for monolingual writers in translingual pedagogies? Would proficiency in translingual writing ultimately benefit our students socially, educationally, and professionally? What might we risk in a translingual writing paradigm? For example, would translingual writing practices erode the fragile connections that heritage language users have to the language of their parents and grandparents? What can we learn when we study models of effective translingual writing (see Ahmad 2007)? As they write, what strategies have "translanguagers" adopted to help their readers interpret their linguistic choices? What choices have they faced in determining the codes and conventions of their text production? What considerations have helped them make their choices? What composing or cognitive stages characterize the production of their translingual writing?

I love Bergeron's idea of "listening to write." When we listen to our voices as we write, Bergeron invites us to imagine an audience of readers and, through a kind of empathy, to hear ourselves through their ears. How will this empathy shape what we write and how we write it? As we ponder the expansive role of writing in the world today – and tomorrow – we have the opportunity to expand our imaginations of who our readers will be; how they will hear what we write; and how, as a consequence, meaning can be shaped, shared, and disseminated.

REFERENCES

Ahmad, Dohra, ed. 2007. *Rotten English: A Literary Anthology.* New York: Norton.

Bergeron, Katherine. 2010. *Voice Lessons: French Mélodie in the Belle Epoque.* New York: Oxford University Press.

Britton, James. 1982. "Writing to Learn and Learning to Write." In *Prospect and Retrospect: Selected Essays of James Britton,* edited by Gordon M. Pradl, 94-111. Montclair, NJ: Boynton/Cook.

Canagarajah, A. Suresh. 2006. "The Place of World Englishes in Composition: Pluralization Continued." *College Composition and Communication* 57, no. 4: 586–619.

———. 2011. "Translanguaging in the Classroom: Emerging Issues for Research and Pedagogy." *Applied Linguistics Review* 2:1–28.

Gilyard, Keith. 1991. *Voices of the Self: A Study of Language Competence.* Detroit, MI: Wayne State University Press.

Graddol, David. 1999. "The Decline of the Native Speaker." *Association Internationale de Linguistique Appliqué Review* 13:57–68.

Horner, Bruce, Min-Zhan Lu, Jacqueline Jones Royster, and John Trimbur. 2011. "Opinion: Language Difference in Writing: Toward a Translingual Approach." *College English* 73, no. 3: 303–21.

Saro-Wiwa, Ken. 2007. "Sozaboy: A Novel in Rotten English." Excerpt in *Rotten English: A Literary Anthology*, edited by Dohra Ahmad, 391–97. New York: Norton.

Trimbur, John. 2008. "The Dartmouth Conference and the Geohistory of the Native Speaker." *College English* 71, no. 2:142–69.

Williams, Raymond. 2001. *The Long Revolution.* Peterborough, ON: Broadview.

IOANA CHITORAN

twelve The Power of Sound and Silence

Katherine Bergeron makes a connection between *sound* and the *written word*, and between *sound* and *silence*. Both she and I study and write about sound. She writes about music while I, as a phonologist, focus on language — specifically, spoken language and the sounds of speech. In both cases, writing is a tool for recording, but the written word or note is really meant to be sounded out. Its true purpose is to not be silent. In my brief response to Bergeron I have chosen to address each of the two associations.

Sound and the Written Word

Bergeron tells us that the power of writing rests on the *voice*. Interestingly, this metaphor was at the center of discussions throughout the 2012 Writing Summit, as we see in the chapters in this volume. Bergeron's contribution is based on her book titled *Voice Lessons* (2010). She urges us to read aloud what we write, to recognize the importance of sounding out the words that we write. She explains: "Writing, like music, is an art of time. When you take the time to read aloud, you change your relationship to what you have written. You become audience to your own thought, grasping its contours in new ways. Listening to your writing allows you to rehearse like a performer — testing your interpretation, shifting the tone, adjusting tempo and rhythm — to bring out the character of your ideas, to get the thinking right."

Likewise, David McCullough exhorts writers to "write for

the ear as well as the eye. Read what you've written aloud, or have someone read it to you. And listen closely. You'll hear mistakes you don't see." Other contributors extended the metaphor. Steven Strogatz notes that he wishes he had Lewis Thomas's voice — by which we understand him to mean Thomas's writing style, the kind of impact he makes through his writing. And Hortense Spillers suggests that "one who would write must position herself in relationship to those shifting currents of enunciation and opinion." This is indeed a powerful metaphor: *we write to be heard; we write to make our ideas heard, to make a difference* — the power of *writing* is, in part, in *sound* and *voice*.

We perceive writing and sound as inextricably linked in communication and the expression of our ideas and emotions. Yet we know that sound and voice are not essential. In signed poetry performances we can see with our eyes the equivalent of sounds like the elusive French vowel that Bergeron refers to, *l'e muet* or the mute *e*, and its shortening or lengthening as a phrase shortens or lengthens, moving along with its prosody.

Sound and Silence

Bergeron's contribution also demonstrates how silence helps hearing and understanding. She asks us to stop after the first period of the Bach piece, to allow us to hear the sentence. This small experiment about the power of the silence in processing what we hear is supported by empirical research in speech perception. Oded Ghitza and Steven Greenberg explored this phenomenon. They took a "speech signal" (2009, 115) — for example, a full sentence — and compressed it until it became unintelligible to human listeners. They then inserted silent intervals within the compressed signal. The intelligibility went back up! It improved the most when the silent intervals were eighty milliseconds long and were inserted periodically. We can interpret their results this way: the insertion of silence in this particular way renders back the intelligibility of speech, because it repackages the signal into portions that correspond to the frequencies of neuronal oscillations observed in decoding normal, unaltered speech.

Bergeron's haunting and rigorous exploration of writing, composing, sound, and silence thus finds its echo in my world of phonological science, reminding us that the power of writing has its sources in far more places than the surface features most traditionally ascribed to it.

REFERENCES

Bergeron, Katherine. 2010. *Voice Lessons: French Mélodie in the Belle Époque*. New York: Oxford University Press.

Ghitza, Oded, and Steven Greenberg. 2009. "On the Possible Role of Brain Rhythms in Speech Perception: Intelligibility of Time-Compressed Speech with Periodic and Aperiodic Insertions of Silence." *Phonetica* 66:113–26.

editors and contributors

Editors

KELLY BLEWETT is a student at the University of Cincinnati, where she is pursuing a PhD in rhetoric and composition. She graduated from Miami University of Ohio in 2005 and worked in a publicity department of Random House before earning her MA from the University of Louisville in 2010. Since then she has taught at Dartmouth College and worked as a research assistant and a freelance writer. Currently she reviews books for her local NPR affiliate, teaches composition courses, and writes a monthly column on motherhood for *Cincinnati Parent*.

CHRISTIANE DONAHUE has been a writing program administrator in the United States in one form or another since 1992. At the same time, she has been a scholar, earning her PhD in linguistics in France. Her work with the French research laboratory THEODILE (Théorie Didactique de la Lecture Ecriture) at l'Université de Lille III and her participation in multiple European research projects, networks, conferences, and collaborations informs her understanding of writing instruction, research, and program development in European contexts. She is the director of the Institute for Writing and Rhetoric at Dartmouth, where she teaches writing and focuses on research about writing, translingualism, cross-cultural comparisons, and research methods.

Contributors

KATHERINE BERGERON became the eleventh president of Connecticut College on January 1, 2014. Bergeron is a passionate teacher, an award-winning scholar and a talented administrator with a record of successful innovation in liberal education. From 2006 to 2013 she served as Brown University's dean of the college, the chief academic officer for undergraduate education, and she is credited with renewing the university's focus on teaching and advising during a period of historic growth. Under her leadership, Brown improved its writing requirement; strengthened the undergraduate concentrations; transformed academic and career advising; bolstered support for underrepresented students; created innovative programs in public service; launched initiatives in online learning; and developed new approaches to undergraduate research, STEM education, and the internationalization of the curriculum. Trained as a music historian, Bergeron was recruited to join Brown University as professor of music in 2004 after twelve years on the faculty at the University of California, Berkeley. She was named chair of the music department at Brown in 2005 and, a year later, appointed dean of the college. Earlier in her career, she taught at Tufts University and at the University of North Carolina at Chapel Hill. Bergeron's interdisciplinary research focuses on French cultural history of the nineteenth and twentieth centuries, with an emphasis on music and language. She is the author and editor of numerous scholarly articles and books, including two prize-winning monographs, *Decadent Enchantments* (University of California Press, 1998), about the revival of Gregorian chant, and *Voice Lessons* (Oxford University Press, 2010), a study of French-language education, linguistic science, and the emergence of the vocal art known as *la mélodie française*. Throughout her career, Bergeron's teaching and research have been enlivened by performance. A singer of eclectic tastes, she has performed Gregorian chant, the blues, the court music of central Java, contemporary pop music, experimental music, and French art song.

PATRICIA BIZZELL is Distinguished Professor of English at the College of the Holy Cross in Worcester, Massachusetts. She founded the college's Writer's Workshop and a program in writing across the curriculum, directed the college's honors and English honors programs, chaired the English Department, and was speaker of the faculty. Bizzell serves on numerous committees and boards, including the board of the "Voices of Democracy: The U.S. Oratory Project" website, funded by the National Endowment for the Humanities, which presents important speeches in American history. She has a BA (summa cum laude) from Wellesley College, a PhD in English literature from Rutgers University, and a master's degree in Judaic studies from Hebrew College. Bizzell has written dozens of essays, articles, book chapters, scholarly papers, and lectures. With Bruce Herzberg she coedited *The Rhetorical Tradition: Readings from Classical Times to the Present*, which won the National Council of Teachers of English Outstanding Book Award in 1992. In 2008 she received the Exemplar Award from the Conference on College Composition and Communication. At Holy Cross she teaches first-year academic writing, rhetoric and public speaking, nineteenth-century American literature, women's literature, and Jewish literature. Among her current projects are essays on Jewish rhetoric and a book on teaching English in South Korea.

LESLIE BUTLER is an associate professor of history at Dartmouth College. She received her doctorate at Yale University and taught at Reed College and James Madison College, Michigan

State University, before coming to Dartmouth in 2003. Her first book, *Critical Americans: Victorian Intellectuals and Transatlantic Liberal Reform*, examines a group of liberal intellectuals who sought to remake public life in the second half of the nineteenth century. Her current project (titled "The Woman Question in the Age of Democracy") explores what debates over women's role in the family, economy, and polity can tell us about political thought in the nineteenth century.

IOANA CHITORAN is a professor of linguistics in the Department of Linguistics at Université Paris 7–Denis Diderot. Previously she was a faculty member in the Program in Linguistics and Cognitive Science and the Department of French and Italian at Dartmouth College. She holds a BA and MA in English and Russian philology from the University of Bucharest, an MA in American studies from Michigan State University, and a PhD in linguistics from Cornell University. Since 2006 she has also been a research affiliate at the Haskins Laboratories at Yale University. Chitoran's work focuses on the interface between phonology (the cognitive representation of sound systems) and phonetics (the physical properties of sounds). She studies how variations in speech can give rise to stable linguistic categories that make up the sound systems of the world's languages. Most recently she has been researching the languages of the Caucasus region, Georgian and Lezgi. In addition to participating in numerous academic committees, conferences, and talks, she has organized such events as the Workshop for Young Linguists: Caucasian Languages (2009, in Lyon, France) and Sounds and Tastes of the Caucasus: Music, Language, and Food in Georgia (2007, sponsored by the Leslie Center for the Humanities and the Dickey Center at Dartmouth College).

KEITH GILYARD is the Edwin Erle Sparks Professor of English and African American Studies at the Pennsylvania State University. His specialties include African American language and literature, rhetoric and composition, and creative writing. Gilyard received a BS in communication and English from the City University of New York, an MFA in creative writing from Columbia University, and a doctoral degree in English education from New York University. He is a former president of the National Council of Teachers of English and a former chair of the Conference on College Composition and Communication, which gave him the Exemplar Award in 2013. The author or editor of seventeen books, Gilyard has received two American Book Awards, one for his 1991 educational memoir, *Voices of the Self: A Study of Language Competence*, and the second for his 2010 biography, *John Oliver Killens: A Life of Black Literary Activism*. In addition to his scholarship, he has published three books of poetry: *American 40*, *Poemographies*, and *How I Figure*. Prior to joining the Penn State faculty in 1999, he taught at Medgar Evers College of the City University of New York and at Syracuse University, where he served as director of the writing program.

JOSEPH HARRIS is an English professor at the University of Delaware, where he directs the composition program and teaches academic writing, critical reading, creative nonfiction, and digital writing. He was the founding director of the Thompson Writing Program at Duke University—an independent, multidisciplinary program noted for its approach to teaching writing as a form of intellectual inquiry. His book *A Teaching Subject: Composition since 1966* (1996, updated 2012) begins with an analysis of the 1966 Dartmouth Seminar. His other books include *Teaching with Student Texts* (2010), *Rewriting: How to Do Things with Texts*

(2006), and *Media Journal* (1998). Harris served as editor of *College Composition and Communication* from 1994 to 1999 and of the Studies in Writing and Rhetoric book series from 2007 to 2012. He is currently at work on *Dead Poets and Wonder Boys*, a book on how the teaching of writing has been depicted in film and fiction. To learn more, visit josephharris.me.

MARIA JERSKEY is an associate professor of education and language acquisition at LaGuardia Community College, City University of New York. A compositionist, she teaches and supports academic writers across the disciplines, ranging from precomposition English as a second language (ESL) or basic writers to postdoctoral scholars. Her scholarship interrogates the legacy of a monolingual paradigm of writing in a translingual world, examines the connections between writing self-efficacy and social pedagogies, and assesses the implications of the writing and publication practices of multilingual scholars. She is the author or coauthor of books, chapters, and articles on the role of language in teaching writing, designing equitable writing programs, and cultivating translingual writing practices. Jerskey also coordinates the Literacy Brokers Program at LaGuardia; serves on the executive editorial board of *College Composition and Communication*, is a member of the Conference on College Composition and Communication's Committee on Second Language Writing; and offers lectures, workshops, and seminars on meeting the needs or building on the resources of culturally and linguistically diverse college writers. Her doctorate in English education is from New York University, and her MA degree in teaching English to speakers of other languages is from Hunter College. Prior to joining LaGuardia's faculty, she served as the founding director of Baruch College's writing center.

MICHAEL MASTANDUNO is the Nelson A. Rockefeller Professor of Government and dean of the faculty at Dartmouth College. He received his PhD in political science from Princeton University in 1985 and joined the Dartmouth faculty in 1987. His areas of research and teaching specialization include international relations, us foreign policy, and the politics of the global economy. His current research concerns the rise of China and its implications for international politics and economics. He is the author or editor of numerous books, including *Economic Containment, Unipolar Politics, International Relations Theory and the Asia-Pacific*, and *us Hegemony and International Organizations*. Mastanduno lectures widely in Europe and Asia and has been a guest faculty member at the Graduate School of Economics and International Relations in Milan, the University of Tokyo, and the Geneva Center for Security Policy. He has been awarded fellowships from the Brookings Institution, the Council of Foreign Relations, the East-West Center, and the Salzburg Seminar. During a sabbatical from Dartmouth, he served as a special assistant in the Office of the us Trade Representative. He is a member of the Council of Foreign Relations and Phi Beta Kappa. Mastanduno served previously as director of Dartmouth's John Sloan Dickey Center for International Understanding and as associate dean for the social sciences. He has received Dartmouth's Distinguished Teaching Award and the Karen Wetterhahn Memorial Award for Distinguished Scholarly Achievement.

DAVID MCCULLOUGH is a celebrated historian, lecturer, and author. Educated at Yale University and widely acclaimed as a master of the art of narrative history, he is a two-time winner of the Pulitzer Prize, two-time winner of the National Book Award, and a recipient of the Presidential Medal of Freedom, the nation's highest civilian award. McCullough's most recent book, *The Greater Journey: Americans in Paris* (2011), was number one on the *New York Times*'s best-seller list. One of his previous works, *1776*, has been deemed a classic, and his 2001 *John Adams*, which has more than three million copies in print, remains one of the most distinguished and widely read American biographies of all time. The book's adaptation as a seven-part HBO miniseries produced by Tom Hanks and starring Paul Giamatti and Laura Linney was one of the most praised and talked-about television events of recent years. McCullough's other books include *The Johnstown Flood, The Great Bridge, The Path between the Seas, Mornings on Horseback, Brave Companions*, and *Truman*, which was made into a television movie by HBO. A gifted speaker and lecturer, McCullough has also been host of public television's *Smithsonian World* and *The American Experience* and the narrator of several films, including Ken Burns's documentary *The Civil War* and the movie *Seabiscuit*. In addition to his other major awards, McCullough has been twice honored with the prestigious Francis Parkman Prize and won the National Book Foundation's Distinguished Contribution to American Letters Award and the National Humanities Medal. He has been elected to the American Academy of Arts and Sciences and the American Academy of Arts and Letters, and he has received forty-seven honorary degrees.

DANIEL ROCKMORE is a professor of mathematics and computer science at Dartmouth College, as well as the director of Dartmouth's Neukom Institute for Computational Science—"a catalyst for interdisciplinary collaboration at Dartmouth using computational science to aid the myriad research projects on campus"—and the William H. Neukom 1964 Distinguished Professor of Computational Science. Rockmore holds a bachelor's degree in mathematics from Princeton University and a PhD in mathematics from Harvard University. His research interests include complex systems, network analysis, machine learning, cultural evolution, and group theoretic transforms. His scientific work and efforts to increase public awareness of science have been supported by the National Science Foundation and the National Institutes of Health, as well as by other agencies and foundations. He is the author of many papers, articles, essays, and lectures. His book *Stalking the Riemann Hypothesis* (longlisted for the Aventis Science Writing Prize) is a nontechnical account of the history of a 150-year-old unsolved math problem. He has a long history of interdisciplinary work that integrates the sciences and the arts, among which is the well-regarded *Music and Computers: A Theoretical and Historical Approach,* an interactive web-based book that he coauthored with, among others, the former Dartmouth professor Larry Polansky. Rockmore has also written about the intersection of math and the visual arts, made four documentary films, reviewed plays and motion pictures for newspapers, been a frequent radio commentator on National Public Radio, and led such lecture series as the First Mind/Brain Symposium at Dartmouth College.

HORTENSE J. SPILLERS is the Gertrude Conaway Vanderbilt Professor of English at Vanderbilt University. Since receiving her PhD from Brandeis, she has taught at Wellesley College, Haverford College, Emory University, and Cornell University. She was also an editor of the *Norton Anthology of African-American Literature.* Spillers has been a guest professor in Duke University's Program in Literature and at the John F. Kennedy Center for North American Studies at the Free University, in Berlin. She is the recipient of numerous honors and awards, including Rockefeller Foundation and Ford Foundation grants. After joining the

Vanderbilt faculty in 2006, she cofounded the *Feminist Wire*, an independent online magazine. She is also the executive director of Vanderbilt's Issues in Critical Investigation, which promotes the intergenerational study of the African diaspora. Her publications include a collection of scholarly essays, *Black, White, and In Color: Essays on American Literature and Culture*. She is the coeditor of *Conjuring: Black Women, Fiction, and Literary Tradition* and the editor of *Comparative American Identities: Race, Sex, and Nationality in the Modern Text*. Her current projects look at black culture, black women, and early state formations, and at Vanderbilt she teaches American and African-American literature, Faulkner, and feminist theory, among other subjects. She delivered the 2010 Sidney Warhaft Distinguished Memorial Lecture at the University of Manitoba and gave the DuBois Lectures at Harvard University in the fall of 2014.

STEVEN STROGATZ is the Jacob Gould Schurman Professor of Applied Mathematics in the Department of Mathematics at Cornell University. He received his bachelor's degree from Princeton University, master's degree from Cambridge University, and PhD in applied mathematics from Harvard University. He was a National Science Foundation postdoctoral fellow at Boston University and Harvard. Prior to taking a faculty position at Cornell, he taught mathematics at the Massachusetts Institute of Technology. The winner of multiple awards, including a lifetime achievement award for the communication of mathematics to the general public, Strogatz works in the areas of nonlinear dynamics and complex systems and is often inspired by everyday life. He may be best known as a coauthor of a 1998 article in *Nature* on small-world networks. Between 1998 and 2008 it was the most highly cited article about networks across all scientific disciplines, and the sixth most highly cited article—on any topic—in all of physics.

In addition, Strogatz has been a frequent guest on National Public Radio's *Radiolab* and wrote a weekly column on mathematics for the *New York Times* in 2010. In addition to numerous scholarly articles, he has written the most widely used textbook in the field, *Nonlinear Dynamics and Chaos*; the best-selling science book *Sync*; the critically acclaimed and popular *The Calculus of Friendship*, chronicling his remarkable thirty-year correspondence with his high-school calculus teacher; and *The Joy of x*.

MELANIE BENSON TAYLOR is an associate professor of Native American studies at Dartmouth College who specializes in us Southern and Native American literature and culture. She is the author of *Disturbing Calculations: The Economics of Identity in Postcolonial Southern Literature, 1912–2002* (2008) and *Reconstructing the Native South: American Indian Literature and the Lost Cause* (2012), both in the University of Georgia Press's New Southern Studies series. She has also published numerous articles and essays examining the intersections of economics and literary culture in modern and contemporary Southern and Native American writing and film by William Faulkner, Barry Hannah, Louis Owens, Randy Redroad, and others. Her current book projects include "Indian Killers," an exploration of violence in contemporary American literature by and about Native American peoples, and "Faulkner's Doom," a study of Faulkner's Indian characters as refractions of economic anxiety in the modern South.

KATHLEEN BLAKE YANCEY is the Kellogg W. Hunt Professor of English and Distinguished Research Professor at Florida State University. She has served in several elected leadership positions, including as president of the National Council of Teachers of English, chair of the Conference on College Composition and Communication, and president of the Council of

Writing Program Administrators. Cofounder of the journal *Assessing Writing*, she co-edited it for seven years; currently, she edits *College Composition and Communication*, the flagship journal in writing studies. She is also cofounder and codirector of the Inter/National Coalition for Electronic Portfolio Research, which has brought together over sixty institutional partners from around the world. She has served on several boards, including the Steering Committee of the 2011 National Assessment of Educational Progress and the Steering Committee for the American Association of Colleges and Universities' Valid Assessment of Learning in Undergraduate Education project. Yancey is the author or coauthor of over ninety articles and chapters and the author or coeditor of twelve scholarly books, including *Delivering College Composition: The Fifth Canon, Electronic Portfolios 2.0,* and *Writing across Contexts: Transfer, Composition, and Sites of Writing* She is the recipient of several awards, including the Florida State University Graduate Mentor Award, the Council of Writing Program Administrators' Best Book Award, and the Donald Murray Writing Prize.

index